# SUPERVISOR'S SURVIVAL KIT

Fourth Edition

Elwood N. Chapman

SRA® PERGAMON  SCIENCE RESEARCH ASSOCIATES, INC.
Chicago, Henley-on-Thames, Sydney, Toronto
A Maxwell Pergamon Publishing Company

| Acquisition Editor | Michael G. Crisp |
| Development Editor | Byron Riggan |
| Text Designer | Judith Olson |
| Illustrator & | |
| Cover Designer | Ralph Mapson |
| Compositor | Graphics West |

**Library of Congress Cataloging in Publication Data**
Chapman, Elwood N.
  Supervisor's survival kit.

  1. Supervision of employees.  2. Personnel
management.  I. Title.
HF5549.C442 1985     658.3′02     85-11799
ISBN 0-574-20780-5

Printed in the United States of America.
10 9 8 7 6

# Contents

# Ideas for Using Supervisor's Survival Kit, Fourth Edition

For the past several years, *Supervisor's Survival Kit* has enjoyed increasing levels of success. A major reason for this popularity is that *Supervisor's Survival Kit* works effectively in a variety of situations. It is comprehensive enough to be used as a text for a formal course—yet brief enough to be useful in a seminar. To increase *Supervisor's Survival Kit's* flexibility, the author has developed support materials which can be useful for a number of different applications. These include:

1. A *Leader's Guide* (13-3781) which provides teaching ideas and tips on the most effective ways to use *Supervisor's Survival Kit*.
2. A *Self-Paced Guide* (13-3782) which in a generic fashion applies the concepts presented in *Supervisor's Survival Kit* to the world of work.
3. A new *Self-Paced Guide for the Office Manager* (13-3783) which deals with situations encountered in an office environment.

Professor Chapman also authored a series of books related to supervisory training. One is his all-time best-seller—*Your Attitude Is Showing: A Primer on Human Relations*. Other titles include:

| | |
|---|---|
| *Your Attitude is Showing, 4/e* | (13-3680) |
| *Self-Paced Guide for Your Attitude Is Showing* | (13-3682) |
| *You and the Automated Office* | (13-3683) |
| *Customer Relations: A One Hour Program* | (13-3684) |
| *Put More Leadership into Your Style* | (13-3710) |

For more information on of any of the above products write Science Research Associates, College and Vocational Studies Division, 155 N. Wacker Drive, Chicago, Illinois 60606.

To order any of Mr. Chapman's best-sellers, fill out the order form on page 207 of this book.

# About the Author

Elwood Chapman, lecturer and business training specialist, is perhaps best known as the author of *Your Attitude Is Showing*, one of the most widely used books in the field of business human relations. Mr. Chapman is an experienced teacher (29 years a professor at Chaffey College and 17 years a lecturer at Claremont Graduate School) and a nationally known consultant. Over the years, Mr. Chapman has written more than a dozen books for several major publishers. His most recent book is *Put More Leadership into Your Style* (SRA) which reflects his lifelong interest in the style and substance of the business world.

# Acknowledgments

I wish to thank my clients for keeping me up to date on the demands placed upon the first-line supervisor. Very special thanks go to the following people for their assistance:

Dr. William Martin, California State Polytechnic University, Pomona, California

Diane Casey, Training Specialist, Sears Savings Bank, Glendale, California

Penny Greenwood, Kaiser Permanente, Los Angeles, California

Marilyn Fowler, Corporate Training Director, Safeway Stores Inc., Oakland, California

I am grateful to the following people for their perceptive reviews and suggested improvements on this edition:

Veronica Micklin, The Institute of Financial Education, Chicago, Illinois

Dr. Paul J. Wolfe II, Dundalk Community College, Dundalk, Maryland;

Thomas Milligan, Marine Midland Bank, Binghampton, New York;

Barbara Powers, Wytheville Community College, Wytheville, Virginia

Finally, the contributions of SRA staff members cannot be overestimated. My sincere thanks go to all of them.

*Elwood N. Chapman*

# From the Editor

Few books ever achieve the success of *Supervisor's Survival Kit*. Since its original publication in 1970, hundreds of thousands of readers have benefitted from this brief, highly practical book. We know that people like *Supervisor's Survival Kit* because they regularly tell us so in unsolicited letters. We also know the book works, because the same customers continue to re-order it.

Perhaps the most amazing thing about SSK is the variety of markets it serves. SRA has customers ranging from vocational high schools through major universities; from tiny companies to those in the top Fortune 500. All seem delighted with the reaction of the reader—whether student or management trainee.

We are proud to introduce the fourth edition. Although the basic content remains the same, SSK has been updated throughout and several new cases have been added. There are new chapters on Staffing and Leadership. Also, there is a brand new component titled *A Self-Paced Guide for the Office Manager*. As with previous editions there is a generic self-paced guide and a leader's guide—plus specific self-paced exercise guides for health care, hospitality, financial services, and supermarket industries.

If you are selecting the *Supervisor's Survival Kit* for the first time, congratulations on your choice. I am confident you will find the fourth edition as stimulating and successful as the previous ones.

I am proud to have been the sponsoring editor for all four editions of this outstanding book and want to thank ''Chap'' for his interest, talent, hard work, enthusiasm and, most of all, his positive attitude during these past fifteen years.

Thanks Chap!

*Michael G. Crisp*

Michael G. Crisp

# Introduction

Someday—if it hasn't happened already—you may become a supervisor and be responsible for the productivity of others. Should this happen, your life will change.

Will you be ready for your new responsibilities? Will you earn the respect of those who work for you? Will those who promoted you be pleased with you? The answers lie in how you go about motivating, appraising, and building relationships with those you supervise, the kind of working climate you create, the quality of the decisions you make, the skill you demonstrate in handling a wide variety of human problems, the way you manage your time, how you set your priorities, and the leadership you put into your supervisory style.

Common sense will help you somewhat in becoming a good supervisor, but to make a really successful transition you will need the kind of help this book provides. It is both a classroom text and an on-the-job guide for the "instant" supervisor who has not had the advantage of formal preparation. It can help make your move into management graceful, rewarding, and permanent, and help you provide the foundation for moving into even more challenging management roles in the future.

At the end of each chapter in this book you will find either a Case Study or a Mini-Game designed to involve you in a realistic management problem. The Case Studies (odd chapters) can be used for discussion, written assignments, or self-instruction. The Mini-Games (even chapters) also can be used as case problems, but they are intended primarily for role playing in the classroom or seminar. A game can be played in fifty minutes or less; instructions are provided.

Cases and games are built around nine different roles that are profiled in detail in the back of the book starting on page 201. PLEASE READ THEM CAREFULLY BEFORE READING ANY OF THE CASES OR PLAYING ANY OF THE MINI-GAMES.

# GETTING INTO SUPERVISION

# Should You Be a Supervisor?

---

*After finishing this chapter, you should be able to (1) write out a minimum of ten characteristics needed by a good supervisor and (2) identify which of these you can develop in yourself.*

---

Patti drove home from her job with a financial institution feeling both elated and troubled. After less than two years with the firm, she had been offered a promotion into a supervisory role. *Should she accept it?* Manuel has been happy as a short-order chef for three years. Yesterday he was offered a position as night manager at a substantial increase in pay. *Should he accept the challenge?* Gerald was surprised when he was invited to apply for a management position with his electronics firm. *Should he leave his highly paid, satisfying skill position for the headaches of management?* Mrs. B re-entered the labor market in the health care industry at the age of forty-three. After less than six months, she has been invited into management. *Should she make the move?* George has been encouraged to start thinking about a supervisory role with his national supermarket chain. *Should he leave the security of his union for the problems of management?*

Whether or not to make the transition into management is a difficult and serious decision. When your opportunity comes, you should weigh both the advantages and disadvantages. Would you be happier as an employee with fewer responsibilities? Which would mean more—the personal satisfaction of being a specialist or the status that comes from being a leader? Some people wouldn't consider becoming supervisors, as you can see by the following comments:

> As a supervisor you are squeezed between a rock and a hard place. You have to please management and at the same time keep your employees happy. It's an impossible situation. No, thanks.

> I've seen too many burned-out supervisors to want the impossible headaches of a supervisor for a few more dollars each week. I'd rather be secure and happy without the pressure and additional income, and my family agrees with me.

> I'm a skilled person who takes pride in and receives pleasure from doing my specialized job well. Why should I abandon a skill it took me years to develop?

**Management Defined**

What is management? Managing is getting things done within an organization through other people. It means guiding people's efforts toward organizational objectives; it means inspiring, communicating, planning organizing, controlling, and evaluating; it means setting goals and moving employees toward them. Management is leadership.

Obviously management is not for everyone. Most employees in all classifications are wise to remain nonmanagers, especially when they do not have the temperament or personality for successful careers as supervisors. But how about you? Should you seriously consider a permanent career in management? Would it satisfy your personal needs and values? Would you achieve greater self-fulfillment? Would you be successful? To help you think it through, try answering the ten questions in the checklist below.

CHECKLIST FOR PROSPECTIVE SUPERVISORS

|  | Yes | No |
|---|---|---|
| 1. Do you consider yourself a highly ambitious person? | ☐ | ☐ |
| 2. Do you sincerely like and have patience with people? | ☐ | ☐ |
| 3. Could you assume the responsibility of decision making? | ☐ | ☐ |

4. Is making more money very important to you?     ☐   ☐

5. Would recognition from others be more important to you than taking pride in doing a detailed job well?     ☐   ☐

6. Would you enjoy learning about psychology and human behavior?     ☐   ☐

7. Would you be happier with more responsibility?     ☐   ☐

8. Would you rather work with problems involving human relationships than with mechanical, computational, creative, clerical, or similar problems?     ☐   ☐

9. Would you make a cooperative member of a management team?     ☐   ☐

10. Do you desire the freedom to do your own planning rather than being told what to do?     ☐   ☐

TOTAL   ☐

This checklist was intended to start you thinking, not to tell you definitely whether or not you should become a supervisor.

If most of your answers are yes, it would appear that the role of supervisor might be attractive and comfortable for you. If, however, you gave yourself more no than yes answers, it would appear (at least at this stage of your life) that you should proceed with caution. Such a checklist also helps by pointing out that there are many deepseated factors involved in such a decision. Here are four that should receive your special attention.

*How deep is your need for recognition?* We may all dream about showing everybody how things should be run, but some people can really be more content with a nonmanagement job because they aren't driven by ambition. How strong is your inner drive to gain recognition from others? Would you be willing to work hard enough to parlay your first job in supervision into a middle or top management position? If you can become a superior beginning supervisor, more responsible management positions will be open to you. In fact, you will be able to go as far as your ambition and management skills will take you. If, however, your need for recognition is easily satisfied—perhaps by good fellowship with your co-workers—you may not be willing to pay the price that management requires. You might be happier as a nonsupervisor.

*How important are people to you?* Most jobs require some contact with people, but the job of supervisor requires much more than most. You must be personnel director, counselor, teacher, and practical psychologist all wrapped up in one. You must learn to work constructively with and accept people who irritate, frustrate, disappoint, and hurt you. You must have a great deal of patience, perception, and compassion. In other words, you must really like people. You can't fake it. Yet, if people are truly important to you, building lasting relationships with those you supervise can be highly rewarding—sometimes more rewarding than the money you make.

*Do you consider yourself a good planner? Are you an organizer?* Supervisors must prepare and implement plans. They must spend quiet periods reorganizing their departments. They must *think ahead.* If you prefer to leave planning to others, you may not be happy as a supervisor.

*Do you have leadership potential?* A supervisor, foreman, department manager, or crew chief is more than anything else a leader. He or she must set the tempo, provide the inspiration, and sometimes nurse the employees along, while at other times exercising harsh discipline and handing out constructive criticism. It is a constant balancing act trying to keep a positive team spirit alive in the department. Although some people seem to have a natural leadership ability, most managers have had to develop their skills through training and experience. Don't worry about whether you have been able to demonstrate your leadership yet—it's the desire that counts. If you feel you have the potential, look ahead with confidence to your role as a supervisor. Opportunities to demonstrate your leadership will come later.

**Advantages of Management**

If you have never been a leader, it may be difficult to predict how you will react or perform in a management role. If you have the slightest interest in finding out what your chances are, why not try? Start preparing now and accept the first opportunity that presents itself. Here are some advantages to consider:

1. Opportunities abound. One out of every nine employee positions is a supervisory or management role, so there must be room for you. The police officer who pounds a beat can prepare to become a sergeant. The registered professional nurse can have a master plan to become a superintendent. The factory worker can aspire to become a foreman. The opportunity to move up is nearly always present for those who are willing to plan ahead and prepare. *The Upper Level Leadership Dearth Theory* states that the further up the management ladder you climb, the fewer qualified people exist for the more responsible roles. Translated, this theory means the further you go, the more opportunity there will be. Also, top leaders are more apt to scramble to another organization, thus leaving more vacancies to be filled.

2. Becoming a supervisor is often the best way to reach a better-than-average income quickly if you don't have a skill or specialty. If you have a general educational background and do not have a trade, specialized skill, or professional or semiprofessional license or certificate, you should seriously consider becoming a supervisor. The opportunities, especially in service organizations, are excellent.

3. Supervisors can learn more because of a greater opportunity to participate in company training. They can attend more classes, read

more, and associate with experts. In fact, supervisors must continue to improve and grow with the company or lose out. Employees might be able to find a little niche where they can hide, but supervisors cannot. *The Bigger Pot Principle* applies here. For example, if you feel your personal growth is restricted as an employee, moving into supervision would be like transplanting a plant to a bigger pot where greater root growth is possible.

4. Supervisors almost always know what is happening within the organization. As a part of the management team, they attend meetings, receive more written communications, and are consulted more often. They are members of the inner circle and have a deeper feeling of involvement with the company.

5. Supervisors are in an ideal position to contribute to the welfare of others. As managers they can go to bat for those who are deserving, counseling those who have lost their courage, and strengthening those whose outlook has become negative.

There are, of course, many other advantages in becoming a manager, but there are also disadvantages, a few of which are listed below. Think about them before making a final commitment.

**Disadvantages of Management**

1. *Problem employees can be difficult.*   As an employee, you have already noticed that some co-workers are problem employees because they cause their supervisors to deal with unusual behavior patterns. Handling confrontations, working with grievances, and doing corrective interviews can be traumatic for some people. Supervisors sometimes find themselves in the middle of such complex human problems. There is no escape.

2. *Expect to be more alone as a supervisor.*   Successful supervisors must isolate themselves to some extent from the employees they supervise. It is impossible to be a supervisor and a close friend at the same time. This means that frequently you must back away when you might rather be a part of the group. You will feel this isolation most when you have had to make an unpopular decision and the people you supervise let you know that you are on the opposite side from them.

3. *You will not receive constant reinforcement from your supervisor.* Management people usually treat other managers differently from the way supervisors treat their employees. As a supervisor you will be expected to support and protect your employees at all times. You must give them day-to-day security and constant personal attention. Do not, however, expect this same treatment from your superior. Because you are a manager, you are expected to be

stronger, so your superior will not feel the same need to reinforce you. He or she will take it for granted that you will provide your own personal confidence and self-motivation and will deal more openly and directly with you.

4. *You may have to change your behavior more than you expect.*   Becoming a supervisor for the first time may be one of the most important things to happen to you in your lifetime. It is a bigger transition than most people expect. In becoming a supervisor, you lay your career and reputation on the line; if you fail, your adjustment to a lower level is brutally difficult and often impossible. The change requires realigning your thinking because your whole approach to your career must be different. Your daily routine, your human relationships, and your self-concept must all change. To underestimate the degree of change that must take place in you is to invite failure.

5. A position as a supervisor could mean longer hours without overtime pay. It might also mean taking extra work home with you.

**The Pressures of Management**

The promises and the pitfalls of management are many. But is there any truth to all this talk that becoming a manager is a sure way to get an ulcer? A first-class ticket to a heart attack? A one-way passage to a nervous breakdown?

This frequently expressed fear—that becoming a manager is injurious to one's physical and mental health because of excessive pressures—is a myth. Management people, in general, are as healthy as those not in management. The supervisor can learn to deal with organizational pressures just as the politician must deal with public pressures. Certainly the job may tax your nervous system a little more than some other kinds of work; and the emotional and mental strain may be greater in some careers than others. Every job has its own special demands. The solution, of course, is to handle the job without letting it become too much of a strain. There are special courses that deal with the subject of stress. Some individuals who are highly self-motivated apply pressure to themselves by setting difficult goals that force them to live up to their potential. Properly controlled, stress increases productivity.

Let's look at an example of one individual who wanted the challenge and involvement of a supervisory role. Hank recently accepted an opportunity to become a supervisor. He is approaching his new assignment with an excellent attitude, as is apparent in this conversation with his friend Bruce:

"I admit that I have many fears about becoming a supervisor. I've never thought of myself as a natural leader and have never really had an opportunity to work under pressure. But I've got to cross over the line sometime or I'll never know whether I can make it. I might as well start now and find out what it's like. I realize the days ahead will be the most critical of my career, even though I will supervise only four people at first.

"I see the whole thing as a sort of laboratory experiment. I'll be able to try out all the principles and techniques of good supervision, and if they work well with four people now, they should work well with four hundred people later. It's my first chance to test my ability as a leader. I feel somewhat like a young senator on his first trip to the capital. I've won the election but now I must prove to myself that I can survive."

"Good way to look at it, Hank," replied Bruce. "I agree with you all the way. If you decide to go the management route, give it all you've got. Be a professional."

**The Prior Image Problem**

Should you decide to make the move into management, understanding the *Prior-Image Predominance Theory* will assist you. Wherever you are now as an employee, those above you may have an image of you built on first impressions. When you first joined the organization, you went through a period of adjustment. You were less confident and less capable than you are now. A prior image based on first impressions is no longer fair to you, and you may need to make special efforts—like new grooming, new confidence, more forthright communication—to change it. You may need to do this even before a supervisory appointment is made, but the process should continue after the announcement so that everyone will sense your new maturity and not treat you unfairly because of a less favorable image established in the past.

**DISCUSSION QUESTIONS**

1.  Is the price of becoming a supervisor too high to pay?

2.  Should a college student who does not have a specific clerical, mechanical, technical, or professional skill take supervision courses leading to a management position? Defend your answer.

3.  Are most managers as happy as the people they supervise?

# Choice*

Mr. Big asked Supervisor Joe to choose one of his employees for promotion. Joe must name a new supervisor for a department similar to his by next week. Joe has narrowed the choice to either Mrs. R or Mr. G but is ambivalent about the final selection. Joe knows that Mrs. R feels she is entitled to the promotion because she leads the department in personal productivity. She is the better choice on the basis of educational background and mental ability, but Joe is not sure that other employees will respond well to her assertive ways and high demands. Mrs. R's relationships with others are not as good as Mr. G's.

Joe also knows that Mr. G believes he is ready to make the move. Having seniority, Mr. G has paid his dues. His ability is sufficiently high, and he might be more sensitive to the needs of employees. Because of Mr. G's military training, however, his brand of leadership might seem too harsh in the softer environment of this organization. Joe must consider one additional factor: Mrs. R seems to have more personal confidence than Mr. G.

No matter what happens, Joe knows he will have a human relations problem with the one not selected. Even so, he wants credit from Mr. Big for providing the most successful candidate.

Supervisor Joe comes to you for advice. Base your choice upon the above data and the interpretation you place on the roles of Mrs. R and Mr. G (as described on pages 204 and 205). Which individual would you select? Upon what factors would you base your decision?

---

*Please turn to page 201 and become acquainted with the roles of Mr. Big, Supervisor Joe, Mr. G, and Mrs. R before analyzing this first case.

# Making the Transition

*Upon completing this chapter, you should be able to write out a specific step-by-step plan outlining your successful transition from the role of an employee to that of a supervisor in the same department.*

Last year Marsha was a quiet, slightly withdrawn teller in a financial institution, today she is an efficient, outgoing manager; last year Craig was a graduate student doing research, today he is an office manager dealing with the problems of over twenty employees. Marsha and Craig have successfully made the most difficult transition of their lives. Last year they were followers—today they are leaders. This could easily happen to you.

You will probably move into your first supervisory position from a nonsupervisory job within the same organization. You may move up

**11**

within the same department or be transferred from another section. Either way, you will have a challenging experience ahead of you. To help you explore this transition, let's look at two examples.

Harry and Ruth, who just completed such a transition, are the same age with very similar personal goals and track records. They became supervisors for the same organization at almost the same time. Their appointments, however, occurred under quite different circumstances.

Since Harry knew about his promotion three months in advance, he was able to prepare for his new responsibilities by taking a supervision course at a nearby college, doing some special reading about management, and working closely as an understudy to the person he was to replace. This preparation was designed to guarantee a smooth transition for both Harry and the organization. Ruth, on the other hand, was a regular employee one day and a supervisor the next. Unlike Harry, who was groomed for his new role, Ruth became an "instant supervisor" with almost no opportunity to prepare.

Why didn't Ruth receive the same training and preparation time as Harry? The answer is simple: management cannot always predict supervisory vacancies caused by resignations, transfers, and promotions. Sudden growth sometimes causes the demand for supervisors to be greater than the supply. As a result, management is often forced to fill slots quickly. Every day remarks like these are being made somewhere:

> I realize, Palmer, that you have been with us for only three months, and haven't had supervisory experience, but because of an emergency situation, we want you to take over the department tomorrow morning.

> It may come as a shock, Susan, because we haven't had a chance to groom you, but we'd rather give you the opportunity than go outside. If you accept, we will give you all the help we can.

> Remember when you came to work, Sam, you said you wanted to be a supervisor within a year? Well, you have made it ahead of schedule. Drop by my office later and we will talk about salary and other details.

Each month men and women of all ages take their first step up the management ladder without preparation. If it happens so often, why all the fuss? *To impress on you that the time to prepare is now.*

No matter what your age, education, or experience, you can't predict what opportunities will present themselves in the future. You can't anticipate when your supervisor will leave her or his job or when some other supervisory opening will occur. You can't predict when your chance will come.

**Your First Step as a Supervisor**   When you move into your first management role, you will want to keep your eyes wide open and, as quickly as possible, get the lay of the land.

Every position of leadership responsibility entails certain unwritten agreements or ground rules of operation.

Are you walking into some sensitive human relations situations you need to know about in advance?

Will you be inheriting a problem employee?

Are there any special legal or safety precautions you need to tune in on?

Is there a significant difference between your leadership style and that of your predecessor?

Should you be apprised of some informal reports or unusual protocol?

Upon what criteria will you be evaluated?

You hope answers to such questions will come automatically from your new superior either before or shortly after you make your transition. But do not depend on it. You may have to uncover some problems and dig up some answers on your own. Some new supervisors make a list of questions similar to those above so that they can get answers in advance and avoid unnecessary initial mistakes.

Even if you do an outstanding job of learning which ropes to jump and which to avoid, there will be other pitfalls to guard against. It is one thing to learn theory and prepare for management, but it's quite another to put that knowledge into practice. No matter how much formal preparation you receive in advance, your first few weeks are the most critical. You must begin on the right foot.

**Recognize that Becoming a Good Supervisor Is Not a Piece of Cake**

Making the move from a follower to a leader is a difficult passage involving behavioral changes on your part and adjustments on the part of those who will work for you. If you underestimate the challenge, you will not live up to your own expectations—let alone those of your superiors.

**How to Survive Your First Few Weeks as a Manager**

To help you survive during your first few weeks as a supervisor, try the ten suggestions presented below. They can help make the difference between a sound, easy transition and a needlessly difficult one that will cause you problems before you can show your real ability. They may get you through the crucial period when people's reactions to you may be the most critical.

Use Your New Power in a Sensitive Manner

You may think it can't happen to you, but sudden authority has a strange way of inflating your feelings of self-importance without your being aware that it is happening. Guard against this by neutralizing your new power with a strong dose of humility. Keep reminding yourself that you are basically the same person you were before you became a supervisor. You must now control the efforts of others, but you do not want to abuse your new authority and create hostility in those who must now look to you for leadership.

**Be Patient with Yourself**

Your first days as a supervisor may be hectic. There will be paperwork and deadlines you didn't expect, meetings that will gobble up your time, and problems you didn't anticipate. At the same time, you may become impatient because you want to try new things right away. Relax. Back away. Try taking the long view. Control your outward behavior to hide any stress and impatience you may feel.

**Decide to be a Professional**

The only way you will be happy as a supervisor is to satisfy yourself that you are good at what you do. Personal pride will come only *after* you feel comfortable with your new role—not before. Recognition from both your employees and superiors will signal your arrival.

**Stay In Close Contact With All Employees**

The temptation to please management by increasing productivity may cause you to be less sensitive to the people in your department and their problems. This would be a serious mistake. Despite all your pressing new responsibilities, it is important that you take time to make personal, positive contacts with each employee in the department during your first few weeks as their supervisor, no matter whether you were promoted from within the department or were brought in from outside. These contacts can be accomplished through brief stand-up conversations, by coffee-break talks, or by invitations to talk things over, depending on the number of employees, the time available, and other circumstances. The purpose of each contact is to let each person know that you appreciate her or him as an individual. It is your responsibility to initiate the contact and build the relationship.

**Make Changes Gradually**

Sudden changes scare many people. Unless management demands immediate changes, it is best to get used to the way the department operates before introducing major innovations. When you are ready to make changes, explain them to the people who will be affected by them.

**Watch the Up Side—Protect the Down Side**

Naturally you will want to satisfy your superiors during your first few weeks because you must earn their support. In doing so, however, be sure to protect those who work in your department. Don't pass on the sudden pressures you feel from above to your people. You must act as a buffer and keep your frustrations and disappointments to yourself if you are to keep a smoothly operating, productive department. Your job is to make the work of those in your department easier, not harder.

**Save Some Planning Time**

The hustle and bustle of being a new supervisor may cause you to spin your wheels and try to operate without a plan. If this happens, you may spend too much time moving in one direction and not enough in another. You might solve one problem only to discover that a problem having a much higher priority has been neglected. Take the time to think and plan. Evaluate yourself and your performance on a day-to-day basis. If you cannot find any time for planning while you are on the job, do it at home.

It is possible that some of your close on-the-job friends might try to capitalize on a previous personal relationship now that you are a supervisor. In other words, they may seek preferential treatment. *Do not permit this to happen.* Your first responsibility as a supervisor is to keep all relationships with your people fair and equal. If you violate this principle at the beginning, you will destroy the respect and confidence you receive from others.

Redefine
Your
Working
Friendships

Previous co-workers with whom you have mature friendships will recognize your new responsibilities and will not expect favoritism. These friendships can continue to be close although both parties may need to redefine their agreements and expend additional energy to keep them in balance. As you adjust to these situations, new standards of integrity on your part may be necessary. Such matters as confidentiality (keeping management matters to yourself), self-control, and personal adherence to company rules come into play.

**New Standards
of Integrity**

Some of your employees may know more about your department than you do. How can you handle this situation? By all means, go to them with questons. Ask their advice and accept it. Involve them in as many decisions as possible. You need their help, especially at the beginning.

Let Your Employees
Help You

Once you become a supervisor, do not become so preoccupied with pleasing everyone that you neglect your education. Do not hesitate to ask necessary questions of your superiors, fellow supervisors, and knowledgeable employees; continue to read and study this book (it is most helpful *after* you become a supervisor); and enroll in any outside courses that are available and important to your success. For example, if you discover your new role is putting extra demands upon you in a specific area such as data processing, then study these skills on the outside while you are performing inside. It is widely accepted among educators that when you can apply what you learn immediately, you are motivated to learn faster, cover more material, and understand it better. Once you are a supervisor, your learning should accelerate, not decline.

Adopt a Learning
Attitude

**Initial Goals as a Supervisor**    More than ever it is a time to read and listen. The new supervisor should attempt to accomplish the following goals during the first two weeks.

(1) Keep the productivity and efficiency of the department at previous levels, with some improvement if possible. (2) Redefine and start building a new, strong relationship with each employee. (3) Start building a strong working relationship with fellow supervisors. (4) Make some progress in the direction of becoming a solid member of the management team. This means starting the process of thinking like a manager and not an employee. (5) No matter how you feel on the inside, stay positive and confident on the outside.

Later you can attempt to accomplish more dramatic results. If the first steps have been successful, your future goals are attainable. If not, your more ambitious goals have been pushed further into the future. First things must come first. The way in which you pace yourself during the first few days will determine to a large degree your long-range success or failure. Let's look at an example of what to avoid.

After two years of waiting, Ron finally became a supervisor with the Acme Department Store. He was given a clothing department with seven full-time employees. He began with great enthusiasm, stirring up the employees, making changes on the run, and generally applying the new-broom technique. Predictably, the immediate results were gratifying. Sales jumped and management was pleased. Ron was the new hero around the store. In a few weeks, however, some problems slowly became evident. First came some rumbles from the employees. Next came the resignation of one long-time employee, followed soon after by another. Finally, sales dropped drastically, and management's enthusiasm for Ron changed to discouragement. They soon realized he had committed the cardinal management sin—he had sacrificed the relationships between himself and the people in his department in order to make a big show with immediate results. He had taken the short view instead of the long, and the price both Ron and the company paid was very high.

When you first become a supervisor, be careful not to create more problems than you solve. Move in with confidence and enthusiasm but keep your eyes wide open and don't destroy relationships instead of building new ones. Create a climate of excitement but don't sacrifice your long-range goals for immediate gains. Remember that it's easier to win popularity than to achieve respect. There are many rungs on the management ladder. If you don't make a smooth transition to the first one, you may never climb the others.

**DISCUSSION QUESTIONS**    1. In moving from the position of a worker to a supervisor, what basic behavioral changes would you be required to make?

2. In making the transition to a supervisor in the same department, how would you go about building a supervisor-employee relationship with an employee you were very friendly with before the switch?

3. If you were a personnel director, how would you communicate with and try to change the attitude of new supervisor who had become too impressed with the power of his or her new position?

# Strategy

### Objective

To evaluate alternatives and choose the best approach to use in taking over a new department.

### Problem

Mrs. R has been promoted and will take over a new department tomorrow. She wants your advice on which of the following basic strategies she should use in meeting her new employees for the first time.

1. Move in openly and freely in a warm and friendly manner. Get personally acquainted with each employee quickly. *Eliminate any hint of a threatening climate.* After using this approach for one week, slowly withdraw and let the employees know you are the boss by forming a friendly but firm discipline line.

2. Move in quietly and stay a discrete distance away from each employee. Make little effort to build personal relationships. Give them time to watch your leadership style from a distance. *Let them discover who is the boss the easy way.* Then, after using this approach for a week, relax a little and slowly attempt to establish warm, friendly relationships to build the same kind of discipline you would try to achieve with strategy 1.

Remember, the problem deals only with which approach Mrs. R should take. Support the strategy that will put her in the best position by the end of her second week.

### Players                                   *(If Mini-Game is used in the classroom.)*

Use only the four management roles (Mr. Big, Supervisor Joe, Mr. X and Ms. Y). Students may draw roles as they enter the classroom; then form a panel in front of the class.

### Procedure

After all players have had time to read and become involved in their roles, a lively twenty-five minute discussion of the problem should take place. Each player must strongly defend and support one strategy or the other during this period. Every player should have an equal opportunity to defend her or his choice. At the end of the discussion all four players vote by secret ballot for either strategy 1 or 2, but they need not vote for the one they defended. Votes are then collected and tallied. Nonplayers as well as players win if they select the strategy that receives the most votes.

## Postgame Discussion

Discuss a possible blend of the two strategies to fit the leadership style of the supervisor involved (in this case Mrs. R).

# HUMAN RELATIONS AND COMMUNICATIONS: THE KEY TO SUCCESSFUL SUPERVISION

# Achieving Productivity through People

*Once you have studied this chapter, you should be able to write out three fundamental reasons why a supervisor must work through people to gain hoped-for productivity and thereby survive.*

As you move successfully from the role of worker to that of supervisor, an amazing transformation will take place in the way you look at things. You will suddenly find yourself more interested in John than in the machine he operates; more concerned with Helen than with the records she keeps; more involved with Hank as an individual than with the work he turns out.

**23**

Your attention will shift from things to people, from the job itself to the person who performs the job. In short, you will need to become people-oriented.

Terms such as human relations, human behavior, motivation, attitude, sensitivity, and leadership style will take on a new meaning. Human understanding will earn the same priority in your scheme of things as job know-how. Helping Roberta increase her productivity will be as important as getting one of your reports out on time. Improving Dick's attitude will command your attention along with production figures, deadlines, and work schedules. Why? Because you must make the shift from a job-centered employee to a people-centered supervisor.

Why is this transition necessary? Why must the new supervisor become so people-oriented? Why must she or he learn to focus attention more on people than on the job itself? The answer lies in a simple, basic truth: *A supervisor gets productivity through people.*

**You Can No Longer Do It Yourself**

The moment you become a supervisor, the production work you do yourself becomes secondary to the relationships you build with the people who do most of the actual work. Even though you may be able to do the job better or faster than those who work for you and even though you would enjoy doing it yourself, you must turn it over to your employees. You must achieve productivity by learning how to direct, train, and motivate others. You can seldom afford the luxury of doing it yourself. In other words, in terms of production work in the department, you'll contribute more by doing less. Here's how the process works.

1. If you remain an employee, you are responsible only for your own job performance and productivity. Your productivity is measured and compared with that of others and that is the end of your concern. As a supervisor, however, you are responsible for the productivity of *everyone* in your department. Consequently, management will no longer be interested in measuring your personal productivity but instead will measure the departmental productivity you achieve.

2. Obviously, you can't increase productivity substantially through your own production. You can't supervise effectively and produce at a high level at the same time—you are only one person, not two or three. Even if you came to work two hours early and left two hours late every day to do production work, the increase in total productivity would not be substantial, and, of course, you couldn't continue at such a pace for long.

3. Therefore, as a supervisor, you can maintain or increase productivity substantially only through others. You cannot do it by yourself. If you don't accept this fact, you'll never be happy as a manager.

When you become a supervisor, you must learn to let the personal satisfaction of working with people replace the satisfaction you previously enjoyed in working with things. Your future is in the hands of those who work for you, so you must take pride in creating the kind of relationships that will motivate people to achieve the productivity you desire. First create the relationships—then work through them to achieve your productivity goals.

Encourage, from those responsible to you, an attitude of respect and trust. Accomplish this by listening and following through on their suggestions, going to bat for them with your superiors, recognizing their individuality, and, above all, demonstrating two-way communication.

**Kinds of Productivity**

Because your future as a supervisor is so dependent on a clear understanding of this principle, the next few pages will be devoted to the facts and theory involved. First, a sound understanding of productivity is important. Productivity is a word dear to the hearts of all managers. And well it should be. Productivity in its broadest meaning is the major purpose of all American business and government organizations and forms the foundation of our profit system. It permits us to compete favorably with other countries and is responsible for all the materials and services we enjoy. Only through the productivity of individuals (and machines operated by individuals) do we achieve our Gross National Product (GNP), the sum total of all tangible goods and services produced in this country during a given period of time. As a supervisor, however, you are concerned with only two kinds of productivity: *individual productivity* and *departmental productivity*.

Individual Productivity

As the term implies, individual productivity is the performance or contribution of one person over a specified period of time. It may mean the amount of materials produced, the ideas contributed, the sales achieved, or the quantity or quality of clerical services rendered. Every job has its own special kind of productivity or contribution. Most jobs, however, will fit into one of the three following classifications.

*Tangible productivity.* The factory worker who operates a machine on an assembly line contributes to the manufacture of the item in a form that can be seen and measured by management, so standards or norms can easily be established. For example, if the average employee produces sixty units per hour, and employee A produces seventy units, then it is easy to measure how far above the standard A's productivity is. In addition to factory work, tangible productivity applies to computer and office occupations, repair jobs, vehicle operation, and many other areas.

*Sales productivity.* A salesperson in a retail store knows how her or his performance compares with others, because management keeps a record of each person's dollar sales per hour. An individual's productivity can also be compared with a norm. For example, if sales amounting to $40 per hour is the standard for salespeople of a given classification, and one woman's sales amount to $50 per hour, her position above the norm is easily measured. However, retail salespeople should not be measured entirely on the basis of dollar sales. Since they must also contribute stock work, housekeeping, and other departmental nonselling functions, their productivity base is larger than selling alone.

*Service productivity.* Many employees who do not produce tangible goods or generate dollar sales perform vital services that contribute a different form of productivity. Most of these services come under the classification of customer relations. For example, telephone operators do not produce anything you can see, nor do they normally sell to customers, yet the services they perform are basic to the company they represent. The same is true of the services provided by police officers, bank tellers, nurses, supermarket checkers, waitresses, postal employees, and many others. Although these intangible forms of productivity are sometimes impossible to measure and compare scientifically with norms, they are important to supervisors and the organizations they represent.

The productivity of all individuals is measured to some extent. If an objective measurement is impossible, a subjective measurement is attempted, perhaps comparing one individual with another. The measurement of individuals is vital to good personnel administration and management and must be accepted as part of employment (see chapter 11). The important thing, of course, is to measure the productivity and not the personality of the individual. The more productivity rather than personality is measured, the more objective and scientific the measurement becomes.

Departmental Productivity

Departmental productivity is the sum total of all productivity (by machines and people) that comes from a department or section within an organization. Like individual productivity it can also be tangible, sales, service, or a combination of these and other forms. Just as one individual is compared with another, so are departments. It is easier, however, to measure the productivity of a department scientifically, because it can usually be reduced to figures and accounting data from which management can make its analysis. The important thing to realize is that department productivity becomes your responsibility the moment you become a supervisor. You must live with the figures, reports, and comparisons on a day-to-day basis. If productivity goes up, you are rewarded; if it goes down, you must come up with some explanations. Your reputation in the company will be tied to the productivity record of your department regardless of how much you contribute individually.

Management is defined as ''planning, organizing, directing, coordinating, and controlling activities to achieve productivity goals.'' From a human relations point of view, this process boils down to specific things you do to get work done through and with other people. No manager or supervisor can do it all alone, and frequently the more tasks he or she does personally, the lower the departmental productivity.

*Construction crew example.*  Gus is a construction foreman in charge of three crews. When his roofing crew fell behind, Gus decided to step in and do some roofing himself in an attempt to set a faster pace by example. After one week little additional progress had been made, and his other two crews were beginning to feel neglected. Gus changed his strategy and invited the roofing crew members to ride with him to the construction site. Commuting with the roofers accomplished two things. First, it saved the crew members transportation costs. Second, it gave Gus some communications time both before and after work. When the crew discovered that there was a penalty clause in the construction contract and that Gus had a difficult problem coordinating all three crews, they pitched in and caught up. The transportation strategy had worked. Gus discovered the importance of communicating and working through others instead of doing it himself.

*Shipping department example.*  Despite the fact that Woody felt he already had more than he could handle, he was given new duties in addition to running the shipping department at the paint factory where he had been a supervisor five years. How could he pitch in during high activity periods to maintain shipping schedules if he had to supervise workers in another section? He decided to lay the cards on the table with his six-person shipping department staff. His basic comment was, ''I've been able in the past to help out during peak periods, but I can no longer do this. In the future it will be up to you to maintain schedules without my personal productivity—unless there is an emergency. How you do this is up to you. If you can come up with some time-saving procedures, I will go along with them.''

Six weeks later, after the crew had made a number of helpful suggestions, shipping schedules were achieved without personal help from Woody, and when one member of the staff resigned, a replacement was not necessary. Woody learned that his crew had not been working up to their potential because they could rely on him to step in and produce during busy periods.

*Sales department example.*   Mabel was invited to take over the shoe department in a major retail store because she had the best selling record. In her efforts to establish a good image, she spent 60 percent of her time acting as a good model on the selling floor instead of supervising the other four salespeople. In less than two weeks she was far behind in her supervisory responsibilities (mostly paperwork), and the other four salespeople were becoming more and more discouraged by Mabel's spectacular sales record.

To survive, Mabel had to make a complete turnaround. She started spending her extra time counseling others on improving their sales techniques, holding short stand-up communications sessions, and complimenting the sales staff on their efforts. When she started working through others to achieve higher sales, productivity began to improve. Mabel had learned that sometimes supervisors do more harm than good by trying to do too much work themselves.

Sometimes greater departmental productivity can be achieved only through the delegation of key duties to others.

*Supermarket example.*   Ramon was so besieged by employees seeking changes in their work schedules that his other responsibilities as manager were neglected. At the advice of his regional manager, Ramon turned the entire staffing matter over to his assistant. Result? Ramon was able to spend more time building good relationships with employees and profits increased.

*Banking example*   Alice, operations officer for a Savings and Loan facility, devoted so much time to training a few people to operate computers that other employees felt neglected. She finally turned computer training over to another. Result? Because she was able to improve relationships, efficiency increased to the point the facility was able to maintain a high level of service with one less employee.

*Healthcare example.*   Frieda, a registered nurse in a long-term healthcare operation, decided to delegate a series of duties to her three ward nurses so that she could devote more time to building relationships with the twenty nurses aides under her supervision. Result? The quality of care increased and costs went down.

Please study the chart on page 29 for a moment. Notice that each employee has an individual productivity gap. This gap represents the difference between what each employee is currently producing and what *could* be produced under ideal conditions. Notice, also, that there is a departmental productivity gap— the difference between what the department is currently producing and what *could* be produced.

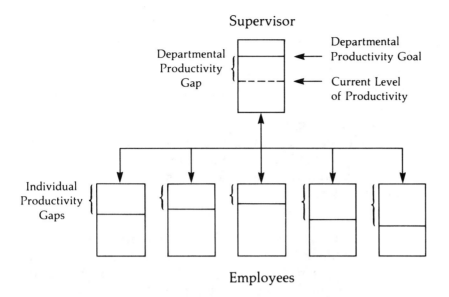

The goal of the supervisor is to close the departmental productivity gap. Because a supervisor can produce only so much as an individual, his or her time should be spent helping employees close their individual productivity gaps. This goal is accomplished primarily through building better human relationships with employees and creating an environment where they will be motivated to reach their own potentials. The remainder of this book will be devoted to helping you learn how to accomplish this goal.

The new supervisor soon learns that there is almost always a difference between an employee's daily performance and his or her capacity to perform. Whether large or small, a productivity gap of some size is natural and should be expected in all employees. Such gaps are, of course, difficult to measure accurately for two reasons: (1) The true potential capacity of an individual cannot really be determined since it is made up of elusive factors such as mental ability, inner drive, perception, attitude, physical stamina, and emotional stability. (2) Job productivity is also difficult to measure. The actual performance of a worker is fluid, moving up and down on an hourly, daily, and weekly basis. At one time an employee can have a very wide gap (anybody can have an off day), while at other times it could be very narrow. In other words, productivity levels quickly move up and down depending upon many internal and environmental factors. The supervisor can control some, but not all, of these factors.

It is only natural that supervisors should be sensitive to changes in productivity levels in their employees. When an employee shows progress in closing the gap between current level of productivity and potential capacity, the supervisor is happy. When the opposite happens, she or he becomes disturbed. The smaller the gaps, the greater the total productivity, and nothing can be more important to the supervisor's personal success. Small wonder the supervisor wants to know every technique that will help to close such gaps.

O.K., you may be saying, I get the picture. I see why I must step in and help my people perform in line with their capabilities. But how do I learn to motivate my people to work more closely to their capacities? How can I increase productivity in my department without more equipment or more employees?

## Motivation Techniques

Many things can happen, either on or off the job, to cause an excellent employee to drop suddenly in personal productivity. In dramatic situations of this nature (when the cause might be highly personal), the supervisor may wish to give the employee a few days to bounce back without interference. But if too much time passes with no improvement, the supervisor should then try to discover the cause and take immediate steps to bring productivity back to the previous level. Hoping that time will take care of the problem can be wishful thinking. Take Bernie for example.

For the past week, Bernie had been producing far beneath his potential as a home-appliance repairman. Most of his co-workers averaged 32 house calls the previous week (average labor billings $1800) while Bernie was averaging only twenty-one calls (average billings $1200). Why? Were Bernie's calls more difficult and time-consuming? Is he less capable, so that it takes him longer? Are there some unknown personal reasons behind the gap between what he is doing and what he could do?

Bernie's supervisor took time to look at his previous record and discovered that Bernie had been above average in productivity until the previous Friday when his productivity gap dropped suddenly to about 50 percent of his normal level. Bernie's supervisor tried to remember any specific event that day that might be the cause. Then it hit him. That was the day the new truck arrived and was assigned to Frank. Was Bernie upset about this? Through a quick counseling session with Bernie, the supervisor verified his hunch. Bernie, thinking he had seniority over Frank, had expected to be assigned the new truck and was understandably upset when he didn't get it—so upset, in fact, that he seriously thought about resigning. In a long heart-to-heart talk, the supervisor was able to satisfy Bernie that his assumption had been wrong and that Frank was entitled to the new truck. The next day Bernie's productivity started going back up. The supervisor had done a successful emergency repair job. Rather than waiting around, he moved in and corrected the situation before Bernie's productivity drop seriously hurt the department or before he resigned.

Communication failures, misunderstandings, and damaged egos are common in most departments, so the supervisor must constantly be on the alert for sudden drops in individual productivity. You cannot always afford to wait to discover whether the problem is job-connected or not.

Not all individual drops in productivity are sudden and dramatic. Sometimes there is a slow deterioration that does not show up for weeks or months. In such instances the supervisor may not be able to find a tangible cause for the widening gap, making corrective action much more difficult. For example, what about the person who has become temporarily disenchanted with the job and the company? What do you do when an employee has temporarily lost sight of a previous goal or has a change in attitude that defies understanding? To illustrate the problem, let's look at the case of Gilbert.

In less than two years with the organization, Gilbert had reached a position of high responsibility in his department. During the past three months, however, there was a noticeable productivity gap. Gilbert's slow loss of drive was reflected in reduced efficiency and generally weaker performance. Gilbert's supervisor decided to try some motivational counseling. She called Gilbert into her office and began as follows:

"Good morning, Gilbert. Thanks for accepting my invitation to drop by. It's been a few months since you and I had a good chat. Tell me, how are things going for you?"

"Well, pretty good I guess. I still like the job and the company okay. I haven't heard any complaints."

"Yes, I still feel you have excellent long-range potential with us. By the way, have you ever thought about where you might like to be in our organization in five years? Do you have a personal goal? Are you, for example, preparing for a job similar to mine?"

"Well, at first when I was really gung-ho, I decided to become a supervisor within three years, but I guess my goals are less crystallized now. Reality is quite different from optimistic first plans, I guess."

The conversation that followed between Gilbert and his supervisor lasted forty minutes. During that time, they had a free exchange of ideas on many subjects, but most of the talk centered on Gilbert's future. At the end, Gilbert admitted that he had lost his focus on a goal, and it had been affecting his work. He expressed his pleasure in getting it all out in the open. It was forty minutes well spent because Gilbert's productivity started going back up within the next few days. In fact, soon it was higher than it had been previously. Before the year was out, Gilbert was promoted to supervisor of another department. Talking things over had apparently restored Gilbert's goal and renewed his personal confidence in his ability to achieve it.

In addition to counseling, there are many other steps you can take to help your employees keep their motivation. First and foremost, keep practicing the five irreplaceable foundations covered in Chapter 5. You can sometimes improve motivation by giving employees special assignments, rotating jobs when feasible, or providing special learning opportunities. Everything you do as a supervisor will have an impact upon the motivation of those who work for you. In turn, the degree of their motivation will determine the productivity level of your department.

**Motivation Theories**

Management books are full of motivational theories. Some, properly interpreted, can be useful to the beginning supervisor. Here are two examples.

From 1927 to 1932 the Western Electric Company conducted what are now known as the ''Hawthorne Experiments.'' These experiments showed that no matter what improvements were made (rest periods, free hot lunches, and so forth) the productivity of the group increased. Why? The employees were made to feel important; just making any improvement gave them more status and respect. Until these experiments, management had accepted as self-evident that the way to improve the rate of production was to improve machinery, provide better lighting, and make similar physical changes. The Hawthorne experiments proved that the emotional climate of the worker is just as important.

Many psychologists claim that employees' inner needs must be satisfied before they can reach their personal potentials. They divide needs into primary and secondary. A primary need is physiological, such as hunger; a secondary need is one that satisfies the mind, ego, or spirit.

**Maslow's Hierarchy of Needs**

One of the best known of such ''need priority'' lists was established by A.H. Maslow.* He ranked needs as follows:

The bottom need is physiological—food, good health. The next is safety and security. The third from the bottom is social needs: one needs to be accepted and enjoy the company of others. Next are ego needs—recognition from others. Finally, at the pinnacle, is one's need for self-fulfillment or self-realization.

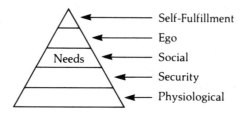

*A.H. Maslow, ''A Theory of Human Motivation,'' *Psychological Review* 50 (1943), pp. 370–96.

The crux of this theory is that the bottom needs must be fulfilled before the others come into play. In other words, you must satisfy your need for food and security before social needs become motivating. You must satisfy social and ego needs before self-fulfillment is possible.

*Suggestion:*   Because the first three levels of your employees' needs are probably already satisfied, concentrate on their ego and self-fulfillment needs. As you implement the basic ideas of this chapter—achieving greater productivity by closing individual productivity gaps—keep these four important principles in mind.

1. Once you become a supervisor, building good relations with employees is more important than being able to do the job skillfully yourself.

   The technical skills you have are very important because you must know how to do something before you can teach and supervise others, but your emphasis as a supervisor will be on transmitting your skills through sound relationships rather than on doing all the tasks yourself.

2. Spending time to restore or improve your relationship with an employee whose productivity has slipped is the most important thing you can do with your time.

   As a supervisor, you will have multiple responsibilities. In all likelihood you will have more things to do than time to do them in, so it will be necessary to sift out and assign suitable priorities to your responsibilities. Top priority should always go to keeping the productivity of others as high as possible. When the productivity of one employee slips, you must be aware of it immediately and begin efforts to do something about it within a reasonable period of time.

3. Management expects you to achieve high productivity from new employees in a hurry.

   Today a faster pay-off is expected from new employees than was true in the past for several reasons: (1) employees have a shorter span of employment today, moving from one job to another more quickly. So, if the mobile employee is going to make a productivity contribution, he or she should do so without wasting any time. (2) The pace inside most organizations is faster today. Orientation periods have been speeded up and training time (both on-the-job and in formal classrooms) is more limited. (3) Training today is more expensive.

   What does this all mean to you as a supervisor? It means you must build relations with new employees as early as possible and

**Supervisor-Employee Relationships and Productivity**

train them quickly so that they reach a good productivity level in a shorter span of time.

4. Your future promotions will be based on the productivity of the people who work for you now.

   Many factors are considered when management promotes a first-line supervisor to a more responsible middle-management position, but nothing influences a favorable decision more than a supervisor's having the human relations skill to get sustained productivity from people. To ignore, underestimate, or downgrade this principle in any way will surely damage your career.

Supervisors occupy a unique and sometimes contradictory role. Although they must possess the knowledge and skills to do a job well, they must refrain from doing it so they can manage. They must be content to teach others how to reach their potential. They must reach their own goals through the efforts of others. It takes a special perspective and sensitivity to accomplish this.

**DISCUSSION QUESTIONS**

1. Why might it be extremely difficult—perhaps impossible—for a worker who has been in a highly skilled job for ten years to become a successful supervisor?

2. When, if ever, would a supervisor be justified in saying, ''It's easier to do it myself?''

3. Does it take as much patience and understanding to be a good supervisor as it does to be a good teacher, coach, or minister?

# Approach

Yesterday Mr. G was promoted to the role of supervisor in a department where customer relations has top priority over everything else. In fact, Mr Big told him he received the promotion because of his outstanding skills with people and his contagious positive attitude.

Mr. G is pleased with the opportunity and hopes that it will be the first step on a path that will bring him additional promotions. He decides on the following takeover approach.

First, he thinks he can eliminate all training in how to handle customers by being an ideal model. He feels strongly that to work well with people an individual must be natural, and he does not want to impose his own customer relations techniques on the personalities of others. He feels that if he sets the pace and becomes a good example, employees will accept the challenge and develop their own style. They will not need specific suggestions from him. He intends to come to work early and stay late to do supervisory paperwork so that he can spend more time out front with customers.

Second, because satisfied employees are the key, he wants to be a "good guy" instead of a disciplinarian. He feels a permissive, relaxed working environment is essential if employees are to be natural and effective with customers. He feels that if he is more accessible to his employees, they will come to him with their problems, and he can develop stronger personal relationships.

Do you see and pitfalls in Mr. G's approach? What changes might you make?

# The Supervisor-Employee Relationship

---

*If you concentrate on this chapter, you should be able to (1) identify the psychological ingredients or factors in a typical supervisor-employee relationship, and (2) write out a specific plan that would enable you (as a supervisor) to achieve a better than average relationship with an employee.*

---

"Sorry to put this additional responsibility on you at this time, but you know how it is. . . ."

"Here's a new report we have to get back to headquarters by Friday even if it means letting something else slide."

"J. B. has called another special meeting for tomorrow afternoon. . . ."

The supervisor soon learns that a constant stream of additional and unexpected time-consuming duties filters down from above. Most supervisors occasionally feel they need more arms and legs and a twenty-four-hour work day to give full attention to their growing list of responsibilities. But no matter how many or how urgent your multiple responsibilities may be, there is one that must take priority over all others: your responsibility to *build and maintain a productive relationship with each employee under your immediate supervision.* No other single responsibility demands the same degree of attention.

Why? As we discovered in the last chapter, building a good relationship with an employee is the best way to close the employee's productivity gap. In addition, only through good relationships combined with strong, sensitive leadership can a cohesive department be built. The *quality* of relationships constitutes the fabric of the department. If relationships fall apart, the whole operation is weakened. If you do not learn to build and maintain these relationships skillfully, your days as a supervisor will be full of turmoil, and you will not reach your potential as a manager.

What is this all-important relationship that exists between the supervisor and each employee? What is its function? How can a productive one be built?

**The Relationship Line**

Perhaps a supervisor-employee relationship is best perceived and understood as a line that exists between the two—a kind of psychological tube or channel through which all communications, reactions, and feelings must flow back and forth.*

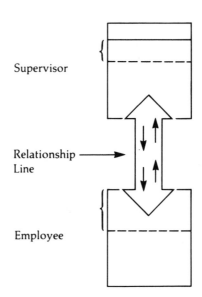

Supervisor

Relationship Line

Employee

---

* E. N. Chapman, Your Attitude Is Showing, 4th ed. (Chicago: Science Research Associates, 1983), Chapter 8.

Through this relationship line each party views, interprets, and reacts to the other. The openness—the amount of freedom or naturalness—of this line contributes to the quality or tone of the relationship which, in turn, is the essence of the working arrangement. Here are three characteristics found in all relationships—these apply to the relationship itself and do not describe the individual at the other end.

*Two-way communication is the lifeblood of the relationship line.* You keep a relationship alive and healthy through an input of words and non-verbal signals from both ends.

Just as all parts of the human body must receive a constant supply of fresh blood to survive, a relationship is kept alive with an exchange of ideas, given strength by words, and kept in good repair through talking. Parties at both ends of the line must contribute. An open dialog keeps the relationship healthy.

The *Mutual Reward Theory (MRT)* states that the relationship between the supervisor and employee is enhanced when there is a good reward exchange between them. For example, the supervisor may provide the employee with freedom to work with minimum supervision, job security, personal recognition, involvement in decision making (all rewards the employee seeks). In return, the employee may provide high personal productivity, dependability, loyalty, and cooperation with co-workers. When such an exchange takes place, both parties benefit. The employee is happy with his or her job; the supervisor is creating a good image with superiors. Without a reasonably good reward exchange, a healthy, productive long-term relationship is difficult to achieve.

*The relationship line can become emotionally charged.* Extreme emotional feelings of either the employee or supervisor can sometimes enter the line and make it very hot to handle. Therefore, you must often take special care in dealing with a highly charged situation. You must go about the work in a quiet, sensitive way. Sparks generated by uncontrolled emotionalism are dangerous to the supervisor-employee relationship. Although both parties share in this responsibility, it is you who must keep the line cool and under control.

You, as the supervisor, are primarily responsible for the condition of any given employee relationship. You must take the initiative to keep it healthy. If it fails, you cannot blame the employee. You need the cooperation of the employee and must assume the responsibility for getting it.

What happens when you fail to build a workable relationship? You create a "problem employee." When this happens there are only two sound solutions. (1) Initiate action to transfer the individual to another supervisor with different leadership style and personality who might be more successful than you. This should be done in all cases where the employee has made a sincere effort to be productive. (2) Consider termination of the employee. This may be the most difficult thing you are called upon to do as a supervisor, but sometimes it is inevitable. More often than not, such action is best for both the employee and the organization. If you should take such action, be sure that all company procedures and policies are honored. In most cases this means checking with the personnel department to make sure that the individual rights of the employee have been protected and that no laws have been violated.

There are many kinds of supervisory jobs. Some supervisors direct large numbers of employees; others only a few. Some work with highly technical equipment; others with customer services. But no matter what the supervisor's scope or the complexity of the job, there can be no greater challenge than building and maintaining healthy relationships with those who look to her or him for leadership. To accept the challenge fully means to plunge deeply into human relations. It means taking a deep, clear look at your own behavior, for one thing is certain: *you get back the kind of behavior you send out.*

**Building Sound Relationships**

Now that you see why you must build and maintain good employee relationships, how will you do it? Listed below are some suggestions.

*See the relationship first and the employee second.* The previous pages have invited you to view the employee through a relationship line in order to become more objective and professional in dealing with employees. By concentrating more on the relationship you will become less involved in the personality of the individual and will probably be less motivated by any unconscious prejudices that you may have. You will also be more scientific in your approach to problems, more aware of your own responsibilities, and more successful in achieving the productivity you seek. This approach also provides an insulation against unwise personal involvements.

When Sylvia first took over the department she dealt only in personalities—attempting to understand and deal with the individual traits of her staff. Resentment developed because her employees thought she was prying into their private lives. Later Sylvia backed away and started to view each worker through the *relationship line* for which she had primary responsibility to keep open and healthy. Not only did this more professional approach build more respect from her staff, but Sylvia felt better about herself because she knew she was more objective and fair.

*Don't play games with relationships.* A relationship is not a toy or game that the supervisor is free to experiment with lightly. Relationships should be honored and treated with deep respect and sensitive consideration. If you hurt the relationship, you hurt the employee. The employee may at times seem too far away to be hurt by your actions, but she or he will most certainly be aware of your attitude.

*Keep all relationships on a business basis.* In most cases, it is best to keep your business and personal lives separate. You may find it hard to have both a working and a personal relationship with the same person (regardless of sex) without losing your objectivity and hurting both your careers. For some people in some situations, a working and social relationship can be combined. However, if either you or those you supervise can't handle this kind of closeness without a distortion of the on-the-job relationship, don't try to blend the two.

*Don't build one relationship at the expense of another.* The goal of the supervisor should be to build and keep relationships with all employees equally. Like the parent of several children, the supervisor should show no favoritism, despite the fact that one employee may need more help than another. In building one relationship, it is easy to neglect others. When this happens, you may become aware of increasingly negative reactions from the other employees. It's similar to the problem faced by the stagecoach driver who attempts to get each of six horses to pull an equal share of the weight at the fastest possible speed over the long haul. It's difficult to hold the reins with just the right touch. To avoid imbalances, the supervisor must occasionally review the state of relationships with all employees in the department. If one relationship has been built at the expense of another, immediate repair work should be the first priority.

*Build your relationship with a new employee quickly and carefully.* When a new employee comes into your department, you have a good opportunity to build a healthy, lasting relationship from scratch. Take time to do this. Do what is necessary to make new employees feel at home, give them the confidence needed to be productive, and help them build sound working relations with the other employees. Do all of this, of course, without being too obvious and hurting your relations with others and without creating a dependency upon you. If you move in quickly and build the right kind of relationship with new employees, they will probably respond with quick productivity, and the relationship itself will last through the many demands made on it later.

*Relationships require daily maintenance.* Just like certain pieces of complex machinery, relationships need daily maintenance. They need to be constantly lubricated with recognition, oiled with attention, and polished with kindness. A good relationship must be protected, nurtured, and closely observed lest it fail because of neglect. Experience shows that the productivity payoff is more than worth the attention.

*Repair damage quickly.* No matter how skillful you become in building relationships, a break now and then is likely to occur. When such disturbances surface, you should quickly make whatever repairs are necessary. Sometimes it means readjusting work loads, schedules, or procedures, or perhaps it requires an apology from you. Whatever it takes, you must move quickly. If the break is beyond repair or requires an outsider, take the problem to your manager or the personnel department.

*In addition to building and maintaining good relationships with employees, you must not neglect relationships with fellow supervisors. The suggestions above are equally applicable as you meet this additional challenge.*

There is a reservoir of specific relationship-building techniques supervisors can employ, depending upon their styles and environments. Near the top of any list should be becoming a good listener. Only when supervisors listen can they discover the special rewards their employees seek that will make the MRT effective; only through listening can problems be identified and solved before they grow into major conflicts that destroy productivity.

Supervisors should remain flexible enough to accommodate harmless personal requests (like leaving early to take care of important personal business) when productivity is maintained and problems with other employees can be avoided. Consistency in style is also significant. Employees do not respond well to supervisors who are unpredictable in their behavior.

Becoming a good one-on-one counselor (Chapter 7) is another skill all supervisors need to master. The list goes on and on, but nothing—absolutely nothing—is more important than application of the five foundations outlined in the next chapter. They can literally make or break you as a supervisor.

**DISCUSSION QUESTIONS**

1. How important is the Mutual Reward Theory in maintaining good relationships between supervisors and employees? Use your personal experiences to support your answer.

2. What are the advantages in successfully separating the relationship between two people from the personalities involved?

3. How much time should the new supervisor devote to building relationships with fellow-supervisors? Are there any precautions that should be taken?

# INTERVENTION

## Objective

To discover the dangers of intervening when an employee's attitude becomes highly negative.

## Problem

Mr. G showed up this morning with a dramatic change in his attitude. Normally positive and pleasant, he is sullen and uncooperative today. Already there are indications that his attitude may hurt the productivity of others. Supervisor Joe has always been proud of the quality of his relationship with Mr. G. He is certain this problem is very personal and not connected with the job. Joe feels he has three possible alternatives for dealing with the situation and he would like your advice. Which should he choose?

1. Immediate intervention through counseling. Nip the problem in the bud by moving in before group productivity suffers.

2. Give Mr. G two or three days to solve his problem before intervening. Even if productivity suffers, he has a right to solve his own problems. He has been an excellent employee. Why take the risk of offending and possibly losing him?

3. No intervention. Mr. G will eventually solve his own problem, and Supervisor Joe should do nothing in the meantime. Supervisors have no right to invade the privacy of employees no matter what happens to productivity.

## Players (For classroom role-playing situations)

Use all four management roles plus Mr. G. All five participants form a panel in front of the class. The role of Mr. G should be assigned in advance to a very perceptive student.

## Procedure

Panel will discuss the three choices for a minimum of twenty minutes. Mr. G plays the key role. He should sit with the panel but remain silent

43

until all players have discussed and voted for one of the three choices. Then Mr. G announces the alternative he feels is best. He should assume that the problem he faces is highly personal and not connected with his job. If you make the same choice as Mr. G, you win.

**Postgame discussion**

Discussion should center around the way Supervisor Joe might intervene without offending Mr. G. The key should come from the individual who plays the role of Mr. G. What were his inner feelings as the problem was discussed? What kind of intervention would he have accepted? When would he be most receptive to intervention?

# Five Irreplaceable Foundations

*Once you have studied this chapter, you should be able to close the book and (1) write out the five foundations for good human relations and (2) describe how you as a supervisor would put them into practice.*

If someone offered you a free formula that would measurably enhance your appearance with little effort on your part, you would be skeptical. It would sound too easy. The same is true with the five foundations presented in this chapter. They sound too good to be true. Yet, these simple, somewhat obvious fundamentals really work and are recognized as irreplaceable by many management experts. They are easy to understand, psychologically healthy, and, although they have been around for a long time, nobody has come up with a more modern or sophisticated substitute that works as well.

**What Are the Five Foundations?**

You will make a serious mistake if you take them lightly. On the other hand, if you weave them deeply into your leadership style, your success as a supervisor is almost guaranteed. Best of all, you can start practicing them immediately.

As a supervisor, you have a certain amount of ''knowledge power.'' You know more about how to perform certain tasks than most of your employees. How you transmit this knowledge is the key to the relationship created.

**1. Give Clear and Complete Instructions**

When such instructions are given clearly and completely, the employee knows exactly what to do and feels good about it; however, when the instructions are hazy and incomplete, the employee loses confidence in the supervisor, and the relationship between them deteriorates. To feel secure the employee must know what is expected and how to do it the best way. This kind of help can come only from the supervisor.

As a supervisor, take time in giving instructions. When possible, use visual illustrations. Follow the basic teaching techniques of keeping things simple and logical and providing examples. Of equal importance, make sure that instructions have been clear and complete by asking for feedback from the employees at the time the instructions are given, and then check the following day to see if the instructions were put into practice correctly. This foundation is so important that a separate chapter will be devoted to it later in the book. (See Chapter 11.)

> With many priority problems facing him, Supervisor Jake nevertheless took time to demonstrate patiently to Mary, an insecure new employee, how to operate a complicated, dangerous machine. Jake gave Mary more than two hours out of his day, including two follow-ups, so that all errors were eliminated. Her second day at work Mary felt completely competent and her productivity was almost up to average. This happened more than a year ago, and Mary has yet to have an accident. Furthermore, Jake has had a strong, sound relationship with Mary from the very start.

**2. Communicate: Let People Know How They Are Doing**

To keep supervisor-employee relationships in good repair, take time to let employees know how they are getting along. Tell them whether or not they are doing well. *But tell them.* Most employees (especially new ones) want to know how to do their jobs better and will welcome help if it is provided in the right way. They also want to know when things are going well and when you are pleased with their performance. Don't let them feel that they are in a vacuum and that you do not care.

Employees respond quickly to any stimuli created by you and can also sense the reaction of fellow employees. But the thing that hurts them most is neglect. They want to feel that they are an important part of the department, and they know that their future depends upon your training and support. The only way to keep the relationship in good working order is to provide both. You are the only source.

Mrs. Browne is a highly capable night supervisor of nurses in an Atlanta hospital. She does not, however, believe in letting people know how they are doing. She almost never tells a nurse when she does well; but she comes down heavy when a violation has been made. As a result, she has more personnel problems than any supervisor on the staff. Nurses are constantly asking to be transferred to other wards. Mrs. Browne has been passed over for a promotion for three years in succession.

Employees need positive reinforcement now and then if they are to keep their personal productivity at a high level. They need the compliment you intended to give before you got too busy with something else; they need the recognition that only you can provide. Look for extraordinary or unusual performance from those who work for you. Sometimes it is best to give credit in front of the entire department. More often, however, it is best given privately. Praise should be given freely, sincerely, and most important, when it is due. To achieve this goal, you must constantly have your radar turned on to observe behavior that is deserving of credit. Supervisors who fail to give credit when due often have standards that are far above those that the employee is capable of reaching and are then afraid that giving credit would be misinterpreted as undeserved flattery. This attitude leaves the employee feeling small and insignificant and usually results in lower productivity. It is necessary to be sincere in giving credit and it is wise to be generous.

**3. Give Credit When Due**

Karen handles certificates of deposit for her bank, which means she frequently deals with senior citizens who have accumulated enough money to purchase them in amounts of $10,000 or more. Many of these people become extremely nervous when making decisions. A few are overtalkative and difficult to send on their way. Others have hearing impairments. Last week at a staff meeting Karen's supervisor complimented the entire staff on the improvements they had made in dealing with these customers and singled out Karen for special mention. The following day Karen told her supervisor that she had been thinking of leaving because she did not feel appreciated, but now she had a new attitude.

There are certain primary problems that only the supervisor can solve. The wise supervisor knows, however, that many secondary problems can be solved through employee participation if he or she gives people the opportunity.

When you involve employees in departmental problems that concern them, you accomplish at least three goals: (1) You give them a chance to learn about the operations of the department, preparing them for future promotions. (2) You build their confidence by providing decision-making opportunities, and, as a result, their productivity increases. (3) You improve the departmental climate by bringing people closer together, thereby reducing friction and misunderstandings. Often the

**4. Involve People in Decisions**

secondary benefits of letting employees come up with solutions to problems are more helpful than the solutions themselves.

When employees help make decisions, they grow and you gain. Involvement makes people feel important, alive, challenged, and stimulated. It can release talent and increase productivity as nothing else can.

Make it a practice to turn over appropriate problems to the people who work for you. Let them struggle with solutions even though you could easily find the answer alone. Once they have an answer, accept it gracefully, giving their solution your full support. Employees often give greater support to their decisions than to those handed down by the supervisor. Do not, however, come up with your own answer and just wait for someone to match it, intending to do what you planned all along. People deeply resent being manipulated in this way.

> Marty, the owner of a successful fashion boutique in an enclosed shopping center, had been paying a free-lance window trimmer to change the front display twice each month. Her three full-time salespeople were so critical of the displays that she asked them to decide whether to keep the professional or to rotate the job among themselves. They said they would like to do it themselves. After two months Marty had to agree that not only were the displays better, but all three salespeople were better motivated.

5. Maintain an
Open-Door
Policy

The supervisor who is easy to approach builds better relationships than the aloof supervisor who is hard to see and difficult to talk with. Encourage your employees to come to you freely with suggestions, complaints, or for counsel. To allow this to happen, you must avoid building physical or psychological barriers between yourself and each employee. Rather, try to establish and practice an open-door policy where free, open, healthy relationships can be built. Fear can prevent good communication. Merely keeping the door to your office open and telling employees to drop by is not enough. You must work to create a nonthreatening atmosphere of welcome that will cause employees to come to you. It's 95 percent attitude and 5 percent policy. (Chapter 7 will be devoted to counseling techniques.)

> Ms. Trent was supervisor of an office staff of twelve. Unfortunately her office was enclosed in glass and visible to all employees. They could not hear Ms. Trent's conferences, but they could observe them. As a result, despite her best efforts, no one wanted to be made conspicuous while talking over problems in the supervisor's office. Her solution was to schedule and conduct short discussions once a month with each employee at a special location in the employee cafeteria. These meetings took time she could ill afford, but it greatly strengthened relationships, and productivity increased.

**Using the Five
Foundations**

These, then, are the five irreplaceable foundations the supervisor can use in building and keeping healthy, productive relationships with employees. Obviously, it doesn't take a mental giant to understand them, nor does it take a supervisor with twenty years of experience to put them into practice. *Why, then, are they so frequently taken for granted and so seldom used?* Here are three possible reasons: (1) Some ambitious supervisors spend their time seeking more sophisticated replacements instead of realizing that these five foundations will serve them well. (2) Some supervisors give these foundations lip service by claiming to use them when in fact they do not. They say one thing and do another— only the people they supervise know the truth. (3) Some supervisors accept the foundations at face value and honestly try to use them but fail because they do not really assimilate them.

How can you sense the need for the five foundations and use them naturally in your daily contact with employees? First, you must make a personal commitment to the five foundations, convincing yourself of their value. You must believe they are sound human relations principles. Second, you must incorporate them into your way of working with your employees, integrating them into your daily routine. You must practice what you believe.

Here is a three-step formula to accomplish this goal.

**Mastering the Five Foundations**

Write out the five foundations on a wallet-sized card. Cut a piece of paper or cardboard to a size that will fit into your wallet without being folded. When you have the card in front of you, write the five foundations in your own words. Turn back to the first part of the chapter if you need to. When you have finished writing all five foundations to your satisfaction, you are ready to continue.

Step 1.

Memorize the five foundations. Holding the card in front of you, take the next five or ten minutes to memorize the five foundations, using any system you wish. (Some people use the "silly word" technique—they devise a five letter meaningless word and build the five foundations around each letter in the word.) You need not memorize the foundations word for word nor learn them in sequence but you should be able to repeat them to yourself without looking at the card. *Without looking at your card,* write them in the spaces below.

Step 2.

(1) _____

(2) _____

(3) _____

(4) _____

(5) _____

Now that you have committed these foundations to memory, repeat them over and over to yourself for the rest of the day in order to fix them in your mind for easy recall at later times. You are now ready for the final step.

Step 3.  Apply the five foundations. If you are currently a supervisor, explain how you plan to apply them during the next two or three weeks with the people you supervise. If you are not yet a supervisor, try to apply the five foundations hypothetically. You might assume that you are Supervisor Joe and explain how you would apply them to the five employees under your supervision.

For this exercise, make any assumptions you wish. Try to be specific. The idea is for you to think through each foundation and then practice using it.

Putting the foundations into practice is similar to learning to type without looking at the keys. It won't be easy and it won't happen overnight, but when it happens, you will be doing almost automatically what so many supervisors only talk about. You will have mastered the skill.

**DISCUSSION QUESTIONS**

1.  Why does the author claim that the five foundations are irreplaceable? Do you agree?

2.  If a new supervisor concentrates only on incorporating the five foundations into his or her daily behavior, will this individual be a good supervisor?

3.  Which of the five foundations would you give top priority? Which one would you give the lowest? Why?

# Request

Mr. Big walked into his office yesterday morning and found a special letter in his in-basket. It reads as follows:

Dear Mr. Big:

Yesterday I received a big shock. My boss, Mr. X, told me he was preparing the necessary papers for my dismissal. I was so upset that I hardly remember what else he said.

When I finally got around to asking him why, he told me that I was habitually late for work in the morning, that I had been warned a number of times, and that he would not tolerate lateness for any reason. I hate to go over his head to you, but I am desperate. It is true that I'm late about fifteen minutes two days a week, but let me give you some background.

I was hired three years ago, after my husband died. I am forty and am the sole support of my three children, the oldest of whom is fourteen. My reason for being late is that I must get my three children off to school. It's not easy. This whole thing never bothered Ms. Y when I was in her department. In fact, she often complimented me and simply asked me to do the best I could about my lateness.

The company has been good to me, and in appreciation I am really dedicated to this job. I work faster and more accurately and waste less time than anyone else in the department despite the fact that I never receive credit and am told how I am doing. I often work through coffee breaks and even part of my lunch hour to make up any time I owe the firm because of occasional lateness.

Would you please review the situation for me?

Sincerely

Jane Pitts

Assuming you are Mr. Big, how would you deal with this problem? It appears that Mr. X may not be practicing the five irreplaceable foundations. Should he be reminded? Should you intervene in behalf of Jane Pitts? Outline the steps you would take.

# Creating a Productive Working Climate

---

*If you deeply involve yourself in this chapter, you should be able to list the steps you would follow (as a supervisor) to create and maintain a productive working climate.*

---

As a supervisor, your attitude is always showing. All the employees in your department have a special kind of radar that permits them to read and evaluate your disposition each day. It gives them a chance to size up and adjust to your present temperature or mood. If you drag into your department with a grouchy, negative attitude, your employees will get the signal and back away from you, going about their jobs with little enthusiasm and avoiding contact with you. If, however, you walk in with a positive attitude, the opposite will happen. They will pick up your outlook, show more enthusiasm, and look for chances to communicate with you.

When you are positive, it's easier for those who work for you to be positive; when you show a sense of humor, it's easier for those who work for you to laugh; when you show confidence, it's easier for others to have a productive day. You set the departmental pace, mood, climate, or ambience.

**The Discipline Line**   The climate you establish is the atmosphere under which employees work—the mood of the working environment. It is also the degree of discipline you maintain. How much freedom do you give your employees? At what point do you put the lid on? Many management specialists refer to this as the *discipline line* and add that supervisors must seek and find their own line based upon their leadership styles. The discipline line is the point beyond which employees know they should not push their supervisor; it is the control point. It defines what employees are permitted to do within the working climate without violating procedures, policy, and working standards.

When a discipline line is too low employees may feel stifled and productivity will drop.

Discipline Line

When a discipline line is too high employees may take advantage of the supervisor and productivity will drop.

A high or permissive discipline line permits maximum freedom because there is a minimum of control or supervision. For the most part, employees are expected to provide their own self-discipline. Such a line works best where employees need great freedom to be creative and no customer contact is involved. A commercial art studio is a workplace where such a line could be successful. Frequently a few employees will tend to take advantage of such an environment.

A middle or intermediate line permits considerable freedom but maintains certain standards that relate to productivity. For example, in a retail store, bank, or airline office, high customer relations standards are maintained, yet the employee is encouraged to be relaxed and friendly. Dress codes are usually enforced.

A low or tight discipline line permits less freedom because it is necessary to protect employees or others. For example, such a line would be required in an atomic plant, where safety is a paramount concern. Rules are enforced by close supervision.

> For her first few weeks as a supervisor, Billie permitted her discipline line to be extremely high and loose. She imposed no standards. When her supervisor complained things were getting out of hand, she lowered (tightened) her line so drastically that her employees were confused and resentful. Billie learned the hard way that oscilating from a wishy-washy line to one that was too tight, or visa versa, is an excellent way to destroy one's career as a supervisor. When it comes to standards, discipline, and control, *consistency* is the name of the game.

The discipline line chosen depends first upon the work environment (art studio, bank, or atomic plant) and second upon the style of the supervisor. Within each environment many variations based upon style will occur. A supervisor, of course, could maintain a low strong discipline line and still have a positive attitude and friendly atmosphere.

Once you find the right discipline line for the work situation, maintaining it will require daily attention. To illustrate, let's look at three hypothetical situations in the same work environment.

> Rick is currently running a rather tight department. His discipline line leaves little room for socializing and a very narrow margin for error. The atmosphere is one of strict compliance. An experienced outsider observing the situation senses that the department might be slightly overcontrolled, overmanaged, and overstructured. The productivity level is *average*.

> Ron, on the other hand, operates a very loose department. He sometimes gives his employees more freedom than they know how to handle. The work gets done, but, because of excessive horseplay, there are occasional errors that must be corrected. Ron feels that employees resent close supervision, so he stays clear except when he feels it necessary to become more involved. The atmosphere is one of noisy relaxation. A trained observer senses an absence of direction. The productivity level is *slightly below average*.

> Susan is following a middle-of-the-road philosophy. The discipline line is there, but it is not overpowering and restrictive. She tries not to be too permissive but consciously avoids overcontrol. As a result, she does a balancing act between the two. She strives to create a democratic climate in which employees have a degree of freedom but still welcome her leadership if and when necessary. To the perceptive outsider, the atmosphere is businesslike with more than average communication between employees. The productivity level is *above average*.

You will recognize that the examples above represent the three classic climates: *autocratic, permissive,* and *democratic.* There are, of course, many variations of each. Although it is estimated that the great majority of working climates fall into the democratic classification, there are working situations where both autocratic and permissive climates are more productive. There are three points to be made: (1) You must create your own departmental working climate. (2) The best climate is the one that generates the greatest productivity. (3) Climates change according to the needs of the department.

**Compassion vs Authority**

The inexperienced newcomer to supervision may think that it is impossible to demonstrate compassion and a tight discipline line at the same time. Not so. Compassion for others can be communicated in *any* working climate. In fact, if handled in a sensitive manner, employees may accept a stronger, lower discipline line from a more compassionate supervisor. Some less-permissive supervisors consistently demonstrate that they care deeply for their staff members. Compassion and authority are not incompatible.

**Developing the Right Climate by Example**

The example you set contributes more than anything else to the working climate in your department. The speed at which you work sets a tempo for others. The friendliness you show toward customers or fellow employees sets a norm for others. The energy and enthusiasm you put into your work is transmitted to those who work for you. Most of your employees expect you to set standards through your personal behavior. They observe your every move: how you answer the telephone, the speed at which you work, and the way you communicate. In other words, as a supervisor, you are always in the spotlight. You are the model.

One of your employees can afford a bad day, but you can't; one of your workers can get by with a grouchy attitude, but you can't; one of your subordinates can let down, but you can't. You are the supervisor and as such you must consistently set the best possible example. It's the price you pay for your leadership role.

**Handling Emergencies**

*The way you handle emergencies shows your real character more than circumstances do.* If you lose your cool under stress, the security of those who work for you will be seriously undermined. Take Marcia as an example.

Marcia was recently hired to manage a government office located on a busy street in a rough section of a major city. She had more than ten men and twenty women working for her, and she knew that she was being tested in many ways. She had not, as yet, been accepted by the staff. One day an automobile crashed through the front window, caught fire, and created general chaos. Marcia handled the situation calmly, efficiently, and without losing her head. From that moment on she was fully accepted as part of the staff.

Marcia's behavior under stress demonstrated her leadership and gave the staff the security it needed. As a result, the working climate became more relaxed and productivity increased. You can't make up a fake emergency to enhance your image with your staff, but when one comes long you can take advantage of it.

Employee mistakes may create some of these emergencies, and the way you react to them is important. Nothing is more deflating to the ego or more embarrassing than to make a stupid mistake in front of others. Yet we all occasionally do it. The way you react to such mistakes by your staff members will greatly affect the climate you are attempting to build. Take Morton for example.

> Morton was the bank manager of a small branch office. He had been in charge only two days when Hazel, carrying a large, heavy tray of coins, slipped on the newly polished floor and spilled everything. After helping Hazel to her feet, Morton calmly got down on his knees and helped retrieve the many coins. He showed no anger, no disgust, no impatience; in fact, he asked one of the other women to take Hazel to the employee's room while he counted and verified her cash drawer. As a result, everybody relaxed and Morton was well on his way to establishing a healthy, productive working climate.
>
> Employees are very sensitive to the way a fellow employee is treated. When Morton built a good relationship with Hazel, he enhanced his relationships with the rest of his staff.

*The way you handle pressures from above affects the working climate.* Every supervisor is occasionally on the receiving end of certain demands from people in higher positions. When this happens, you can react in one of two ways: you can pass the pressure on by calling a staff meeting and chewing everybody out, or you can absorb as much of the pressure as possible without passing it on. Here's the way Steve, a section manager in a large factory, reacted.

Absorbing Pressures

> It was Steve's first job as a supervisor, and in his anxiety to accomplish many things in the first two weeks, he had neglected to have his staff do the necessary cleaning up. As a result, the section was dirty and messy. Predictably, a high level manager made a routine inspection late one afternoon and reprimanded Steve privately—and emphatically—for the condition of his area. Although he was emotionally upset and was tempted to chew out his staff (after all, it was their fault), he absorbed the pressure and said nothing that day. The following morning Steve discovered his staff was busy cleaning things up. Apparently someone had heard the reprimand Steve had received and passed the word along. Steve never had to say a word to his staff. They respected his willingness to take a beating on their behalf, without passing it on. From then on, Steve had little trouble keeping a clean and tidy department.

| | |
|---|---|
| **Communicating Changes** | *The way you react to changes and communicate them to your staff is critical to a productive working climate.* Changes, as we shall learn in Chapter 18, constitute a challenge to the supervisor. In fact, organizational changes are the source of most pressures felt by management and nonmanagement alike. The better you are at adjusting to change, the easier it will be for your employees to accept changes, and the more productive your climate will be. Even more important is the manner in which you communicate forthcoming changes to your employees. |

> Doreen received word Friday evening after all of her employees had left for the weekend that her department would be transferred to an older, less desirable building. She took time on Saturday to inspect the new location and work out a tentative floor plan. She announced the change in a positive way Monday morning and asked employees for input on her plan. Before the day was over everyone had made a good adjustment, and some were looking forward to the additional freedom that would result from being more isolated.

How can you tell when you've created the ideal discipline line or working climate? The best gauge you have is productivity (measured by sales, production units, or service standards). If productivity is up and consistent, you have probably achieved the right balance. If productivity is down, something must be wrong. Other barometers to indicate an unsatisfactory climate are excessive complaints, human relations problems, absenteeism, employee rip-offs, hostility, errors, and a general lack of enthusiasm. Like a custodian controlling the temperature in a room, the supervisor should occasionally take readings and make adjustments.

The major reasons for the deterioration of formerly productive departments are neglect, failure to alleviate controllable pressures, and a discipline line that is too permissive for the situation. Generally speaking, a supervisor with a very high, loose discipline has more problem employees. Employees need a great deal of self-discipline to operate under such conditions. Many are unable to discipline themselves.

| | |
|---|---|
| **Monitoring Your Discipline Line** | You can't maintain a good working climate without giving it some personal attention. You must work at it daily by contributing new ideas and lively comments, injecting a little humor to keep employees reacting in positive ways, inserting some deserved compliments to help motivate people, and, above all, communicating. Obviously, you must do a great deal of testing and experimenting before coming up with a satisfactory climate. Don't expect immediate results. Even after you have achieved a good climate it is not easily maintained. Constant work is required. However, the supervisor who eventually does create and maintain an effective working climate can thereby establish good productivity |

records and enhance his or her personal progress. Here are some suggestions to keep in mind as you work toward this goal.

Err on the side of strong leadership. Regardless of how negatively employees react to a disciplined climate, most would prefer strong leadership (firmer lines) to weak leadership. Most employees cannot function well in an atmosphere void of leadership and direction. They want decisive leadership and work best in a predictable, controlled environment. A lower, tighter line is better than one that frustrates part of your workforce. The fewer rules the better in most situations, but the rules must be clear and set a firm, clear line that all perceive correctly.

*Advantages of a Low, Firm Line*

Joyce moved in as the new store manager quietly and in a warm and friendly manner, but she set a much firmer discipline line than her predecessor. Productivity (measured in sales) was up 20 percent the first month. Later some of her employees told her what it was like to work under the previous manager: "I didn't feel like I was headed anywhere." "There was little satisfaction in doing good work." "Time goes much faster under your supervision." "If there is anything that frustrates me, it's a manager who doesn't lead."

Find the ideal climate for your department and then maintain it. Be consistent in the way you treat your employees and predictable in the way you handle your duties as a supervisor. Daily inconsistency keeps everyone on edge and holds productivity down.

*Consistency Is the Key*

Raymond, an operations manager for a branch bank, set his discipline line on a daily basis. When he was in a light mood, he was extremely friendly and tolerant (raising the line); when he was in a serious mood, he was stern and demanding (lowering the line). In less than two months he had lost two employees, and two others had requested transfers. When asked why, one replied, "He expects us to adjust to his mood every day and we never know just what to expect. He's inconsistent and unpredictable. It's worse than dealing with your own children." Another employee said, "Once you get used to the rules, he changes them in a capricious manner that leaves me disturbed and angry. I would prefer a less capable but more consistent manager."

One way to get feedback from your staff is to mingle a little with your employees during breaks. If the timing seems right, ask how things are going and then listen to the responses you receive. If time is going fast for your people, you are probably on target; if not, you need to make some adjustments. If you receive few complaints, you probably have the kind of climate you want; if you receive many complaints, things must be out of balance, and you should adjust your discipline line. It's easier to make small adjustments to a working climate than to make major repairs.

*Seek Feedback from Employees*

Fine-Tune Your Discipline Line

Adjust your discipline line frequently and gently. Maintaining the right discipline line or climate takes sensitive maneuvering. The supervisor who overreacts one way or the other often must start from scratch. Here is a classic example.

About three months ago things were going well in Carl's department. Production was high. Morale was great. Apparently Carl had come up with the perfect climate, so he relaxed and became more permissive. He felt he could trust his staff. Two weeks later things began to go wrong. Productivity dropped and mistakes increased. Carl, overreacting, moved in and tightened the discipline line harshly and emotionally, resulting in even lower productivity. Employees didn't want to work hard for someone who gave them freedom one day and took it away the next. Carl needed to learn that sudden, drastic adjustments to his discipline line can easily boomerang. The best policy is to take frequent soundings and make minor adjustments.

Maintain a Lively Climate

Lighten the climate with fun and games. It's easy for the supervisor, weighed down with many responsibilities, to become too serious about the job. When this happens, a cloud of gloom settles over the department and everything seems out of tune. The sensitive supervisor, seeing this situation beginning to develop, will break it up with a little fun or appropriate horseplay to deliberately change the mood. Take Odie's situation as an example.

Odie operated a highly successful fast-food franchise. Most of his employees were part-time high school and college students. Knowing that he could pay only minimum wages but needed dependability and high performance, he did everything possible to make the work fun and status-building among the employee's peers, who were frequently customers. Odie was so successful in building enthusiasm that tensions would build and personality clashes would occur. To relieve such tensions, Odie would permit an occasional "snow fight" among employees after the store was closed. Everyone, including Odie, would throw ice (snow) at everyone else for ten minutes, then all would pitch in and clean up the mess. His comments to me were: "It is nothing more than a human relations safety valve that permits everyone to let their hair down harmlessly for a short period. It releases the pressure and helps me keep the working climate I need to be successful."

Keep Employees Challenged

Employ the Chapman Attitude Principle. This principle states that employees, generally speaking, have more positive attitudes when they are busy. Idle workers usually become bored and eventually negative. By keeping employees busy through advanced planning and delegating, the supervisor will create a more positive working climate and reach higher levels of productivity. The most difficult job in the world is one in which there is too little to do. The effective supervisor will see that no such jobs exist under his or her direction.

The most disastrous thing you can do as a supervisor is to break off communication with your people. This usually happens when managers get so busy with reports, planning, research, and other activities that they stay hidden in their offices too much. Loss of communication—for any reason—will destroy morale and productivity faster than anything else. It is only through daily communication that you can measure the atmosphere and decide if you need to adjust your discipline line. Because of this, some supervisors force themselves to get away from their other responsibilities once each day for the purpose of casual communications with their employees. It is a sound investment.

**Communicate Daily**

The ideal working climate is one that creates self-motivation in workers. It is generally recognized today that in most work environments traditional motivational techniques are not working well. Supervisors get little response from most workers through pep talks, contests, pay increases, and traditional forms of counseling. In a large number of cases a worker is either self-motivated or not motivated at all. The contemporary supervisor is challenged to create a climate where, without prodding, workers will want to achieve. In short, employees "catch" motivation from the surrounding climate, a climate created primarily by the way the supervisor supervises. When an atmosphere of confidence and involvement is created, the worker feels good about his or her role and wants to reach out to achieve. Creating and holding onto such a climate is one of the most difficult challenges both new and experienced supervisors face.

**An Ideal Climate Encourages Self-Motivation**

1.  Do different instructors create different learning climates in their classrooms and lecture halls? Under what kind of climate do you learn the best?

2.  Can you give an example of a supervisor whose discipline line is either too firm or too lax, resulting in low productivity?

3.  Do you agree that compassion and strong discipline are compatible? Defend your position.

**DISCUSSION QUESTIONS**

# Climate

### Objective

To gain insight into causes of poor employee morale and to learn ways to restore a productive climate in a demoralized department.

### Problem

Supervisor Joe has just returned from a very disturbing private conference with Mr. Big where he was told that his department productivity had dropped more than 20 percent in the past sixty days. Mr. Big didn't pull any punches. Either Joe must get employee morale and productivity back up or he will be replaced. Joe is very upset. He feels that he has been very considerate with his employees and that they are letting him down. He knows that things have been going badly in the department. Productivity is down; morale is low; griping is high; mistakes have been too frequent. What should he do? After considerable soul-searching Joe comes up with ten steps he might take to restore a healthy working climate in the department. (See list on the following pages). Joe wants advice to help him determine which steps would help and which might do more harm than good. (Readers not involved in group role-playing are invited to go directly to the list.)

## Player

All nine roles should be drawn. Those with management roles constitute group 1; those with employee roles make up group 2. All others in class constitute group 3. The teacher should appoint a chairperson for each group.

## Procedure

All three groups spend twenty minutes doing the following: (1) Eliminate those steps that might do more harm than good. (2) List those left and number them in order of preference. (3) If possible, come up with an action that the group prefers over any of those listed.

Once finished, each group should put its list on the blackboard. Take ten minutes to discuss differences. Everyone then votes for the list they feel will be most effective in getting productivity back up to the previous level. You win if you vote with the majority.

## Postgame Discussion

Discussion should center on: (1) differences among the answers of the three groups, (2) whether any formula would actually restore high productivity, and (3) what caused the department to become demoralized.

Joe's List of Proposed Actions

1. Call a fifteen-minute departmental meeting. Release the productivity figures and make it clear that you expect immediate improvement.

2. Instead of group meeting, take time to counsel each of the five employees on the matter privately. If an employee's productivity is down, be frank about it; if it is mediocre, discuss what can be done to improve it; if productivity is good, be complimentary.

3. Say nothing but start tightening the department by your actions. Set a more disciplined climate without talking about it.

4. Start immediately to correct all violations or unacceptable behavior you spot through private conferences in your office. Be pleasant but firm.

5. Withdraw and act hurt until the employees feel sorry for you and, as a result, come around.

6. Start involving your employees in selected departmental problems that you previously handled by yourself.

7. Have an off-the-job party at your home for all five employees.

8. Give each employee a written report of the productivity drop and ask for written feedback on what might be done to get back to previous productivity levels.

9. Go to Mr. Big with this list and ask him for suggestions.

10. Spend more time with employees, listening to their complaints, working beside them, having coffee with them during breaks, and generally circulating to improve communications.

# Counseling or Communicating Privately

---

*If you concentrate on this chapter, you should be able to (1) eliminate any fears you may have regarding one-to-one counseling, (2) write out the five conditions under which counseling can be effective, and (3) apply the conditions and techniques professionally to an actual situation.*

---

"It's a mistake to teach the first-line supervisor to counsel the employees in his or her department," said Barbara Crane, training director. "Counseling is a tool for professionals only. In the hands of the regular supervisor it could do more harm than good. Besides, the word *counseling* sounds too psychological and scares the supervisor off."

"I disagree, Barbara," replied William Carroll, the personnel director. "If properly understood, counseling can be the supervisor's most effective tool.

All supervisors counsel whether or not they know it, because counseling is nothing more than talking things over. I don't want to make psychologists, psychiatrists, or even professional counselors out of department heads. I just want them to build and maintain productive relationships by talking things over with employees in the right way. In my book, that's counseling.''

This chapter supports the view expressed by the personnel director. Call it counseling, interviewing, advice giving, guiding, or simply communicating privately—it's a major tool in your kit.

The supervisor is charged with the responsibility of keeping all relationships with employees healthy and productive. The best way to do this is to have a sound program of preventive maintenance based on good communication, fair treatment, and other widely accepted human relations practices. But no matter how good the maintenance program may be, any given relationship can become strained, hostile, indifferent, hurt, out of balance, or weak. When this happens, the supervisor must diagnose the problem, prescribe the solution and administer it. The best remedy for a poor supervisor-employee relationship is counseling or talking things over. Counseling, initiated and conducted skillfully, can strengthen a weak relationship when nothing else works.

## What Is On-the-Job Counseling?

On-the-job counseling is a controlled, two-way conversation under optimum conditions. It involves sitting down in some quiet place and getting job problems out in the open without hurting each other—talking, listening, trying to understand the other person's point of view. It involves working out solutions that people can live with. The structure of counseling sessions varies widely. Sometimes a long heart-to-heart talk is needed to clear the air. Sometimes a quick exchange will clear up a misunderstanding. Perhaps the supervisor does most of the talking; the next time it may be the other way around. Counseling is more than a casual discussion resulting from an accidental encounter. Rather, it is serious, two-way, private communication initiated by either the employee or the supervisor to deal with a problem or goal. The purpose of on-the-job counseling is to increase productivity by solving problems and strengthening or repairing working relationships. It's not designed to solve personal or psychological problems. As a supervisor, you are not a psychiatrist, a psychologist, or a professional counselor, but you can counsel employees in your department in order to create and maintain relationships affecting departmental productivity. All other kinds of counseling should be off-limits.

On-the-job counseling, or private communications, usually takes place under one of two circumstances: (1) when the employee voluntarily comes to the supervisor with a suggestion, problem, or grievance, or (2) when the supervisor intervenes to motivate an employee, correct a problem, or forestall a grievance.

The supervisor has the advantage when the employee initiates the discussion. For one thing, it means the open-door policy is working and confidence has been established. Even when the employee approaches in a hostile mood, the supervisor should welcome the communication because talking things over may be the only safety valve available. Most of the time, employees will approach the supervisor without hostility. The climate will then be relaxed and nonthreatening to both parties. These off-the-cuff sessions can do much to strengthen relationships further. The more the employee initiates counseling, the better.

Most of the time, however, the supervisor must initiate the process. Intervention by the supervisor is necessary when situations develop that are hurting the productivity of the department. Naturally, intervention counseling is a sensitive procedure. It takes a good sense of timing, a smooth approach, and enough personal confidence to get things started. Because of this sensitivity, little of it is done. The following statements express the problem:

It's dynamite to move in on some of these sticky human problems. No, thanks. If time can't solve 'em, don't expect me to.

I'm always available to talk things over with the employees in my department if they come to me, but I'm not going to rock the boat by going to them and stirring up more trouble. It's hard enough to keep the lid on this department the way it is.

I work so closely with my people that I communicate constantly on an informal stand-up basis. If I called someone into my office and closed the door, he'd be too scared to talk.

There are obviously many reasons supervisors avoid intervention counseling even when they know that it could solve problems and increase departmental productivity. The most common reason is fear of the unknown.

The purpose of this chapter is to dissipate your fears about counseling and demonstrate that you can and should use counseling frequently and comfortably. There's no magic to performing good on-the-job counseling. You can start right away without fear or misgivings if you understand and use the following principles. They are known as the five R's of counseling: the right purpose, the right time, the right place, the right approach, and the right techniques. Once you learn these principles, counseling will be one of the most important tools in your supervisor's survival kit.

**The Five R's of Counseling**

Counseling as presented in this chapter should be used only for the specific purposes listed below. The supervisor must not exploit the techniques to pry into employees' lives or for other nonbusiness purposes.

The Right Purpose

1. *To strengthen, maintain, or restore a working relationship between you and one of your employees.*   The primary job of the supervisor is to keep relationships healthy, and private communication is the best tool to do this. It should be used, however, only when the break in the relationship has caused a drop in productivity. Let's look at Mr. K as an example.

   Supervisor Joe asked Mr. K to work overtime one Friday night and in the process Mr. K wasn't given a chance to reply that he had promised to take his son to a scholarship banquet. Afterward, Mr. K said nothing, but his attitude changed and his productivity dropped. In talking privately with Mr. K, Joe was able to find out what was wrong, apologize, and restore the relationship.

2. *To motivate employees to greater productivity.*   Counseling can sometimes help a new employee bring productivity up to standard or help more experienced employees increase their productivity. In other words, employees can be motivated to improve through the counseling process. Supervisor Joe's communication with Ricardo shows how this can work.

   Ricardo had done an excellent job for four months as a part-time employee. Then he started arriving late, making mistakes, and otherwise interrupting the smooth operation of the department. Supervisor Joe moved in with a fifteen-minute counseling session. He discovered that Ricardo had been so involved with a personal problem that he had lost sight of his goal, which was to earn enough money to finish college. As a result of the discussion with Supervisor Joe, Ricardo was able to focus once again on his goal and his part-time job became important again. His productivity was soon back up to its normal level.

3. *To resolve personality conflicts.*   Horizontal working relationships between two employees in the same department can sometimes deteriorate, causing emotional conflicts and a drop in productivity. In order to protect both the department and other employees, it is sometimes wise for the supervisor to move in with counseling. The "Mrs. R vs. Mrs. Q" incident is a case in point.

   Mrs. R had made the mistake of badgering Mrs. Q about her productivity, and Mrs. Q had reacted by sulking and letting her productivity drop below standard. Supervisor Joe heard the rumble and invited Mrs. R to talk it over. The basis for the approach was that he was responsible for Mrs. Q's productivity and that Mrs. R (because of her maturity and ability) should take the initiative (with Joe's help) to restore the injured horizontal relationship. The repair work took time and required much outside support from Joe, but this approach worked.

4. *To discipline an employee.* Skillful counseling is the best possible tool to use in correcting employee violations of rules, procedures, or policy. It's a sensitive task to discipline others but when it must be done, counseling is more effective than an emotional chewing-out in which everybody in the department hears the verbal exchange. Supervisor Joe used this technique effectively to correct one bad habit and enabled Mrs. Q to save face.

Mrs. Q was socializing too much with other employees, overstaying her coffee breaks, and discussing nonbusiness matters over the telephone with other employees. Supervisor Joe was inclined to be tolerant until he noticed her activities were affecting the productivity of others. Then he invited Mrs. Q into what became a twenty-minute counseling session. Joe stated his concerns quickly but was careful not to show any hostility. He also gave Mrs. Q a chance to defend some of her actions. The period ended with a positive exchange by both parties. After two weeks Joe was pleased with the way Mrs. Q had curtailed her socializing.

5. *Orientation and termination counseling.* Counseling is an outstanding tool to use with a new employee until she or he is fully adjusted and has survived the probation period. Many supervisors set up a formal counseling period with new employees during the first day on the job, at the end of the first week, and at the end of the first month. Private communication is also the best approach when the supervisor must terminate someone. Such a session is never easy, of course, but handled properly it can substantially help the employee, the supervisor, and the company. Supervisor Joe was forced to terminate an employee some months ago. Rather than handling it on a cold, one-way basis, he took the time to discuss it at length with the employee in a counseling environment. The employee left the company in a better frame of mind, and, of course, Joe felt better himself.

Because counseling is always a sensitive process, the timing (usually under the control of the supervisor) is vitally important to a successful outcome. If the timing is right, the results can be excellent. If the timing is wrong, little may be accomplished. Here are four suggestions that should help you choose the right time.

**The Right Time**

1. *Do not intervene with counseling until you are sure it is necessary.* Every employee has a few bad days or a temporary struggle with his or her attitude. Use counseling only after productivity has been down for a number of days, and you are confident nothing else will solve the problem. Premature counseling can do more harm than good.

2. *Don't initiate a counseling period when you are upset, frustrated, or angry yourself.* Remember—counseling is a two-way affair, and if you use that opportunity to get rid of some inner hostility, it will kill any chance of a successful session.

3. *Certain times of the day are not conducive to effective counseling.* Peak activity periods, just before lunch, and just before the end of the day (when employees may be anxious to get home or meet appointments) are not the most suitable. Also, try to avoid periods when the employee may be upset emotionally unless the cause of the upset is the reason for the counseling.

4. *Do not set up a counseling session too far in advance.* If you invite an employee to meet you in your office at 2:00 P.M. when it is only 10:00 A.M., he or she has four hours to worry and get upset and probably will produce at a lower rate. In almost all cases it is better to set a time with either a short gap or none at all.

The Right Place
Having the right place for private communication can be more important than you think. It's almost impossible to do successful stand-up counseling or to accomplish much in a noisy place where there are frequent distractions. The ideal situation, of course, is a private office. Some supervisors, however, must settle or less. One solution is coffee-break counseling, providing outsiders don't interfere. Another alternative is to make arrangements to use somebody else's office or a vacant room.

The Right Approach
The major reason supervisors back away from problem counseling is that they are afraid of the first hurdle, the approach. They think about it and plan it, but not knowing how to take the first step prevents them from executing their plans. There are at least four primary causes for this hesitation:

1. Fear of saying the wrong thing at the beginning, thereby causing an unpleasant confrontation
2. Fear of invading the employee's privacy
3. Fear of opening up a hornet's nest of other problems
4. Fear of being disliked by the employee

Most of these fears are not substantiated by fact. Employees like to talk to their supervisors, even about unpleasant matters. Employees do not always resent being disciplined, if done in the right way, and often admit that help was needed even though they would not ask for it.

To get past these fears, supervisors simply need a formula or procedure to follow. The following procedure is suggested if you have a difficult employee problem to face. (1) Invite the person into your office or other designated place without advance notice so there will not be time to build fears and create a threatening climate. (2) Start the conversation quickly and don't beat around the bush. Try saying something like this: "We have something rather unpleasant to talk about but we will both feel better if we get at it." (3) State facts only. Do not make accusations. Try to keep a calm, pleasant, subdued voice. Encourage the employee to talk. Don't rush.

As you develop your own formula, one that fits your personality, you'll find that it is not difficult to launch even a potentially unpleasant counseling session.

There are two basic types of counseling, *directive* and *nondirective*. In directive counseling the supervisor does most of the talking and draws a rather firm line on the direction the interview will take. Although the supervisor should use this approach in a gentle and quiet manner (constructive counseling ends when an argument begins), the employee should sense that advice or direction is being given. Communication in these sessions is mostly from the supervisor to the employee. This technique is usually considered best for the following kinds of situations:

**The Right Techniques**

1. When there is a violation of company rules or policies
2. When mistakes need to be corrected
3. When employee hostility (toward you, others, or the company) has reached a stage where it can no longer be tolerated

Nondirective counseling is almost the opposite. The supervisor does less talking and encourages the employee to communicate more. It's a soft approach designed to bring hidden problems out into the open or to set a climate for free and constructive discussion on any matter important to the employee. The permissive, unstructured, or open type of counseling is often very therapeutic and provides motivation for the employee. It is the only technique to use for positive counseling when no problem exists and is considered the best approach for the following kinds of situations:

1. When an employee appears to have lost her or his touch or positive attitude over a sustained period of time, resulting in lower productivity
2. When you want to strengthen or restore a relationship
3. When you feel you can motivate an employee to greater productivity

**MRT
Counseling
and the
Non-Directive
Technique**

The Mutual Reward Theory (page 39) functions well when the rewards are sufficient and well balanced between supervisor and employee because both parties come out ahead. The employee gets rewards from the supervisor and the supervisor receives high productivity and subsequent recognition from superiors. When such rewards are insufficient or out of balance—or the wrong rewards have been provided—MRT counseling may be the answer. When a supervisor takes time to sit down with an employee and work out a sound, reasonable reward exchange, improved motivation is almost predictable. This can happen best under the non-directive approach because the employee is more apt to openly state those rewards desired. The two cases that follow illustrate the technique and the approach.

Jerry had watched Mildred's productivity deteriorate for three months. In addition, her co-workers were now complaining that she was not carrying her part of the work load. Jerry called Mildred into his private office and in a very quiet, non-directive manner said, ''Mildred, there are certain rewards I can give you as an employee. There are also rewards you can give to me as your supervisor. Would you be willing to discuss them?'' During the next forty minutes they developed a practical reward exchange and outlined it on a piece of paper. Jerry was careful to agree to only those rewards that he could actually provide. He made certain that the rewards he requested from Mildred were reasonable. This arrangement turned out to be mutually rewarding. It was clear the following day that Mildred would quickly regain the motivation she had when she was first employed. By using MRT counseling Jerry had rebuilt a relationship that improved productivity in his department.

Martin, a management trainee for a hotel chain, had been assigned to Sandra's department for thirty days as part of an extended training period. After he had been in the department two days, Sandra gave him a special assignment that involved some research and a written report. Although it was turned in on time, the report did not live up to Sandra's expectations or reflect Martin's high potential. Sandra decided to use the soft, laid-back, approach to MRT counseling. After some small talk about a humorous incident that had occured earlier in the day, Sandra said:
''Martin, I realize you will be with me only one more week, and I appreciate having you; but I am a little concerned about your future. I want you to learn everything possible while you are here. Would you permit me to propose an arrangement whereby we both can come out ahead for the final week? For example, if you will write down three job-connected rewards you would like to receive from me this week, I will write down three rewards I would like to receive from you. We can then openly discuss them. Is it a deal?''
Twenty minutes later they had carved out a reward exchange that was easy for Sandra to implement. It guaranteed that Martin's last week in her department would be productive.

MRT counseling offers unusual opportunity to the supervisor who is willing to sit down and forge out a simple reward exchange system with an employee. It could be the most motivating technique in your survival kit.

*As a supervisor you should use nondirective counseling much more than directive.* If you find you are not, you may be using counseling primarily to put out fires instead of considering it as a positive way to strengthen relationships, increase productivity, and prevent problems from developing. Generally speaking, the more you use the nondirective technique, the less you need the directive.

Of course, the way you use either approach really determines its effectiveness. Here are some techniques that will help in both situations:

1. A quiet voice is more effective and less threatening than a loud voice.
2. A good way to dissipate the employee's hostility is to let him or her talk it out.
3. When the employee is talking (perhaps defending some action), listen instead of planning your rebuttal.
4. Periods of silence in a counseling interview can help the employee do some important self-evaluation so don't rush to break in on them.
5. Free and honest communication is restricted when a time limit is imposed or implied.
6. Since most abuse coming from employees is directed toward the system, the organization, or themselves, try not to take negative comments personally.
7. The resolution of a problem is not the only sign of a successful counseling period. The mere act of achieving two-way communication is worthwhile.
8. Attempt to end all sessions on a positive note and, if necessary, schedule a follow-up meeting.

**Link All Counseling to Individual Goals**

For maximum effectiveness, all counseling sessions should be tied to the employee's goals. The supervisor may be required to help the employee re-establish previous goals or establish new ones.

Maggie, a registered nurse who supervised the maternity ward on the night shift, was having trouble with Marty, a vocational nurse in charge of cleanup procedures. Marty wanted to take over the R.N.'s responsibilities instead of performing her own tasks. When Maggie discovered, through counseling, that Marty was taking college courses leading to R.N. certification, she modified her approach. She agreed to give Marty extra duties that would help in her advanced training—providing she took care of her other, more mundane responsibilities first. This concession immediately improved the relationship.

Surveys made in large organizations show undisputed evidence that the higher up the management ladder a person travels, the more time she or he must spend counseling others. Some company presidents spend up to 80 percent of their time in private communications with their executives. Without question, counseling is a tool the ambitious supervisor cannot ignore.

**DISCUSSION QUESTIONS**

1.  What additional reasons might explain why supervisors are so reluctant to initiate private communication sessions with their employees? What would you suggest to a supervisor who has this problem?

2.  Some management and personnel people claim that young supervisors today find it more difficult to do counseling, especially for discipline or termination, than their older counterparts. Do you agree or disagree? Why?

3.  Does frequent stand-up or informal communication between a supervisor and an employee eliminate the need for private or formal counseling? Build your case one way or the other.

# Technique

Supervisor Joe is upset over the night watchman's written report (sent through Mr. Big's office) accusing Ricardo of goofing off on the job and of (on one occasion) having a woman friend at work with him. The situation is aggravated by the fact that Supervisor Joe recently defended Ricardo in front of Mr. Big, who had used him as an example when accusing Joe of being too soft with his employees. In checking further, Joe also discovers that the stockroom (one of Ricardo's responsibilities) is in very poor condition. Joe concludes that Ricardo is taking advantage of him. He decides to have a serious talk with Ricardo this afternoon when he reports to work after his last class at college. Joe is aware that Ricardo is highly sensitive, unpredictable, and sometimes explosive. He also recognizes that Ricardo has been a productive employee in the past and has high potential. His problem is deciding between the two counseling techniques.

*Technique 1: Directive counseling.* Under this firm approach Joe would force an unpleasant confrontation by laying all the cards on the table in a stiff warning designed to shake up Ricardo. There would be no possibility of misinterpretation. Ricardo will know exactly where he stands, and the session would amount to a first warning that could lead to termination.

*Technique 2: Nondirective counseling.* Under this softer approach Joe would try to avoid an unpleasant confrontation by talking things over easily and quietly so that in the end Ricardo would discipline himself. Joe would try to listen more than talk—he would be sensitive to Ricardo's explanation. In this manner Joe would gain better results in the end and avoid harsh words that would be mutually disturbing.

Which technique would you use? Why? If you select an alternate approach or a combination of the two, defend your position.

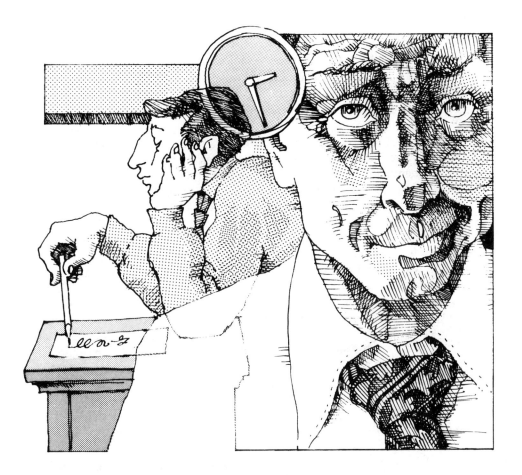

# The Problem Employee

*This chapter will give you the skills you need to deal confidently with problem employees.*

A problem employee is one who repeatedly violates a departmental discipline line, frequently causes disturbances among other personnel, or lowers productivity through some form of unacceptable behavior. Sooner or later every supervisor must deal with such an employee. A manager does not have the luxury of letting time take care of such individuals, and you cannot sweep them under the carpet.

Counseling (interviewing) is the answer and the techniques covered in the previous chapter will come to your rescue. Through counseling, a skillful supervisor is often able to turn a problem employee into a superior employee by discovering the cause and coming up with the

77

right answer. Sometimes, however, the best a supervisor can do is alleviate the problem so that everyone can live with it and productivity is not damaged. In some cases the only acceptable solution is to take corrective measures, which may end with the dismissal of the employee. Every case deserves individual analysis and treatment.

Diane, a single parent, was demonstrating an increasing amount of hostility toward working with her fellow-employees. So much so, that departmental productivity was measurably down. After two counseling sessions, the problem was narrowed down to an imbalance between home and career. Diane was unable to separate the two and, as a result, she was laying home problems on top of job demands. This resulted in behavior that irritated co-workers, created customer complaints, and put unreasonable demands on her supervisor. Once the situation was isolated and discussed, Diane was able to discipline herself into a better home-career balance. She was no longer a "problem employee."

Chris was a classic example of how the frustration-aggression hypothesis can create a problem employee. A recent graduate from an MBA program, Chris had set excessively high career goals for himself. As a result he became frustrated over his slow progress and this, in turn, resulted in aggressive behavior. For example, Chris would lose his patience in working with others and walk away in a huff. During staff meetings he would seek controversy and spill out his feelings. After two counseling sessions, Chris recognized his own problem and found employment in a new environment where his talents and education could be put to more immediate use.

## A Professional Perspective

What are some of the fundamentals involved? What are the mandated corrective steps? And, most important, how can you prepare now to handle such individuals?

First, you should keep the following five fundamentals in mind so that you view the individual—and the problems he or she is creating—in professional perspective.

## Expect Good Results

*Have faith in your ability to resolve the problem and build a better relationship with the individual.* You must initiate communication with the problem employee if the problem itself is to be dealt with openly and a solution reached. If you fear the process, you are already at a disadvantage. Keep in mind that counseling is basically talking things over in private. The more you use and upgrade your counseling skills in nondiscipline situations, the more effective you will be with corrective interviews.

## Everyone Can Come Out Ahead

*Accept the premise that there is probably one solution that is best for the individual, you, and the firm.* The only way you can get to this elegant solution is through counseling. Your goal is to save the employee, keep him or her in your department, and convert the individual into a productive, nondisturbing, member of your team. The more you anticipate good results the more they are apt to occur.

*Recognize that heavy discipline at the beginning often intensifies an existing problem.* Both you and the employee may have a tendency to be defensive. If you create a threatening climate, the employee may become emotional. The problem employee becomes more of a problem and a solution becomes impossible. Another reason why a heavy hand at the beginning can backfire is that heavy discipline can, perhaps through misinterpretation, cause other employees to feel uncomfortable.

Nondirective Counseling May Be Best

*The longer one waits to correct unacceptable behavior, the more explosive the interview may become.* Most supervisors who delay taking action permit the behavior of the problem employee to get under their skin, where it festers until the supervisor can no longer deal with it objectively. The sooner you deal with a problem, the less emotional you will be.

Waiting Is Usually a Mistake

Jason tolerated Rosemary's disruptive behavior for six weeks without saying a word. Each time she violated his discipline line his dislike for her increased; each time she was insensitive to customers and co-workers he became more frustrated. Finally, one morning he reached his tolerance level, invited her into his office, and exploded. The moment the interview was over Jason knew he had made several mistakes. His relationship with Rosemary worsened and he could not see any chance in the future to restore it. He had a guilty feeling about his behavior and he knew it had hurt his relationships with co-workers. He was ineffective for the rest of the day. As a result, Jason resolved to deal with such problems as soon as they surface in the future.

*Accept the fact that a single problem employee can cause your downfall as a supervisor.* The following case illustrates this fundamental.

Protect Yourself

Some co-workers did not think that Marge was ready for her promotion to operations officer of her busy savings and loan establishment. But management thought differently, and their confidence in her seemed justified, at least during the first months. A serious cloud appeared when Susan, a teller, became a problem. It started when Susan violated the acceptable dress code; it intensified when she became sullen with some customers; it became intolerable when it affected the productivity of others. Although Marge had no experience in handling such a situation, she knew she had only three alternatives. She could delay action, she could go to her boss, or she could initiate a one-on-one talk today. She decided on the last and immediately called Susan into her office.

Marge was careful not to create a threatening climate. She did not overplay her hand, but she quickly led into the problem and made it clear that she was in charge and was going to stand her ground. Although there were some difficult moments, eventually some healthy two-way communication took place. Susan decided that the work environment in a savings and loan was not for her, and one week later she resigned. Susan departed without hostility, and Marge had solved her problem. From that moment on, all of her employees seemed to respect her more, and productivity increased. Best of all, management was most complimentary. Her immediate superior said, ''We were monitoring the situation carefully and sensed that your future depended upon how you handled Susan. We are extremely pleased.''

Objectivity Required

Even if you accept the above fundamentals and practice them, solving employee problems will not be easy. Many, however, are less difficult than they appear. One reason is that an employee may become a ''problem'' in your eyes but not in the view of others. The employee is irritating you but not co-workers or other management personnel.

Roger had a solid reputation as a superior manager but he became irritated with Tony, a management trainee, the first day Tony was assigned to his department. Roger thought Tony was too aggressive. He immediately disciplined Tony in unfair, unprofessional ways—not his usual attitude. Then, by chance, he overheard two of his regular employees defending Tony. Roger took stock of himself, admitted he had been unfair, and made a complete turnabout. As a result, he built an excellent relationship with Tony. What he had interpreted as aggressiveness was assertiveness that others appreciated.

Your discipline or authority line is essential so that employees will not only respect you but also keep their productivity at a high level. Discipline must be maintained at all costs. But the supervisor must be careful to treat all employees fairly and consistently. There is no room for personal vendettas between a supervisor and an employee.

The supervisor must protect his or her discipline line in quiet, effective ways or eventually lose the respect of those who must live with it. To permit one employee to cross the line is to lose the respect of those who still honor it. When the supervisor loses authority, productivity can drop drastically.

Joel had been able to maintain a relaxed, comfortable discipline line for almost six months. Not a single employee was taking advantage of him. Then Victoria, who was having personal problems, started testing the line from all directions. She not only challenged traditional procedures she had previously honored, but she started to make complaints to Joel's boss. Then the conflict came to a head when she challenged Joel openly on a procedural matter in a staff meeting.

Joel initiated a long interview the following day to discuss her recent behavior in relationship with departmental productivity. The atmosphere was tense until, near the end of the interview, the conversation turned to Victoria's career goal, and Joel stated that he would like to help her reach it. Eventually a kind of trade-off took place; Victoria promised to be more sensitive to Joel and departmental objectives; Joel agreed to do what he could to prepare her for her career goal without favoring her over others. The compatibility contract lasted until Victoria earned a promotion six months later.

The purpose of the exploratory interview is to get the problem out on the table in a nonthreatening manner. Both parties should have an equal chance to communicate; both old and new facts should be introduced; if possible, the roots of the problem should be revealed. *Sometimes the exploratory interview can do it all.*

Sally took Jennifer out to lunch to discover, if possible, what was causing her hostility. She found a private place, made certain the environment was relaxed, and then introduced the subject. The discussion that followed showed that Jennifer thought Sally had been unfair to her and that her resentment had created a barrier between them. As a result, she had violated the departmental discipline line to show her independence. When Sally convinced Jennifer that the unfair treatment had not been intended, they both agreed to start from scratch. The exploratory interview had solved the problem. No further action was necessary.

Construction superintendent Rich had received two reports that Betty, the woman who did cleanup work in the completed buildings, had violated safety regulations. He called her into his mobile office and quickly introduced the subject. It turned out that Betty was uninformed about the safety regulations and had not been aware that she was breaking them. When there were no further complaints, Rich figured the exploratory interview had corrected the problem.

When the exploratory interview tells the supervisor that the problem is deep, a follow-up is indicated. Such a follow-up can take one of two courses. In cases where there is evidence that firm rules have been broken, the supervisor initiates a series of corrective interviews. In cases where the human relations problems are complex, one or more noncorrective follow-up discussions may be necessary to resolve the problem. The decision to conduct follow-up interviews can be made during the exploratory interview or later. The supervisor can discuss it with the employee in advance or use the wait-and-see approach. Each case requires individual analysis. Sometimes the exploratory interview is interpreted by the problem employee as a warning—sometimes it is not.

Assume that during an exploratory interview you suspect a problem employee is violating a rule, but you have no evidence. Later, however, you discover the evidence. At that point you set up corrective interview 1.

*Corrective interview 1.*  The purpose of this first follow-up step is to verify the violation and warn the employee. Verification means *Critical Documentation.* Although required documentation varies among organizations, basically it should include (1) a specific description of the violation; (2) the name of the violator, the date it occurred, and the date of the corrective interview; and (3) the written acknowledgment or rebuttal of the employee. Corrective interview 1 is, in effect, a documented first warning.

*Corrective interview 2.* This interview need not take place unless a further violation is reported. If a second incident (even a different violation) is reported, the second interview should take place with the same documentation procedure. This meeting becomes a second warning.

*Corrective interview 3.* This interview is necessary only if a third violation occurs. The procedure will vary according to each organization (and legal counsel) but generally will include (1) a third person (upper management person, personnel director, or staff lawyer); (2) a review and presentation of previous documented warnings; and (3) notice of termination. Whatever the exact procedure, the supervisor should permit two-way communication and attempt to show the employee that he or she has been treated fairly. The rights of the employee must be protected at all costs.

When the above procedure is followed carefully most employees will submit their resignation voluntarily before corrective interview 3 takes place.

**Noncorrective Interviews**

Assume that during an exploratory interview you discover a deepseated human-relations problem. Perhaps a personality conflict between two co-workers is damaging productivity. Maybe one employee's attitude is so negative that it is hurting the productivity of others or causing customer complaints. Possibly there is a conflict between you and the problem employee. Situations of this nature call for one or two follow-up interviews.

*Noncorrective follow-up 1.* A single exploratory interview will not solve most human problems. It takes time to dissipate misunderstandings and misinterpretations. When an exploratory interview reveals hostility between the supervisor and an employee, for example, the conflict may never be solved. But holding one or two follow-up interviews is more effective than trying once and giving up.

Jane was disturbed to discover that Carol was upset and hostile toward her. About all she was able to accomplish during the exploratory interview was to listen and let Carol get her inner anxieties and frustrations out in the open. Three days later Jane conducted a follow-up interview that was less volatile, and there was more of a two-way discussion. At this stage both individuals admitted to some mistakes and misinterpretations. The relationship was beginning to rebuild. Later Jane initiated a third interview in which mutual rewards were discussed. Eventually the relationship was fully restored and all hostility dissipated.

*Noncorrective follow-up 2.* As illustrated above, more than one follow-up interview is often necessary to solve a human relations problem. The process of restoration is not easy or fast. In most cases, some give and take is necessary to build a new foundation for mutual respect. Normally some behavioral changes must take place on both sides in the interim between interviews. The supervisor should not expect to be able to solve all human problems, but in most cases the combination of good exploratory techniques plus one or more follow-up interviews will be an excellent investment to ensure harmony and high productivity in a department.

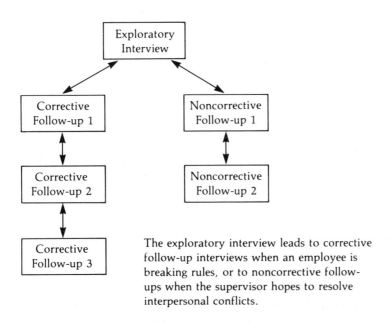

The exploratory interview leads to corrective follow-up interviews when an employee is breaking rules, or to noncorrective follow-ups when the supervisor hopes to resolve interpersonal conflicts.

Give the interview process a chance to work. Inexperienced supervisors sometimes becomes discouraged if they do not see immediate results. Resolving conflicts, helping others change their attitudes, and dissipating hostility takes time. Remind yourself that, although the process does not always work, it works often enough to be worth your effort. Even if you fail, you will have had the satisfaction of trying.

The best time to build a healthy, rewarding working relationship is when the employee first comes under your supervision. If you can build respect early, create a relationship that is fair and mutually rewarding, and then maintain it, you will usually be able to avoid trouble.

Preventing Problems: An Ongoing Process

*The way you introduce new employees into your department can forestall serious problems.* You may or may not have the authority to reject a new employee assigned to your department, but the way you receive the new employee is important. Take time to introduce the newcomer to the complete staff, provide a sponsor, and talk about productivity goals.

If you build a strong relationship from the beginning, you will seldom have trouble with the individual later on.

*You may have to learn to live with certain low-level employees.* You may discover one or more employees in your department who do not, and never will, live up to your expectations. These individuals do not influence the productivity of others or cross your discipline line, but they contribute less than other workers. For example, you might have a mature employee who has seniority but cannot adjust quickly to dramatic changes, or an employee who refuses to communicate but produces better than average work. Such employees can make your job as supervisor more difficult, but they are not troublemakers.

Sometimes counseling will strengthen these employees; sometimes it won't. When you have done your best to change behavior, you must continue to be positive with these employees without letting them pull you down or hurt your leadership ability.

*Your image as a supervisor is being tested.* A problem employee can cause a great deal of conversation both inside and outside your department. If you wind up with such an employee, you can rest assured others will be watching how you respond. The nonproblem employees on your staff will be watching even more closely than management. Studies show that most co-workers have a lower tolerance level to problem employees than supervisors expect. Your employees want you to solve the problem to make life easier for them. Obviously, the supervisor who has enough leadership ability to solve the problem will enhance her or his image in all directions.

Keep in mind that you are probably more important to your organization than the problem employee in question, so don't let the individual destroy you. This means you must deal with the employee in legal ways so that both you and the organization are protected. If you need backup assistance, do not hesitate to ask for advice and support from your superiors. As a beginning supervisor, you are not supposed to know all the answers, so do not let personal pride keep you from seeking support. In dealing with problem employees, it can be a serious mistake to act prematurely on your own.

This chapter has been designed to give you the confidence, techniques, and procedures that will help you either prevent employee problems or handle them gracefully and legally when they emerge. If you can handle problem employees effectively without turning to your superiors for help, you will not become their "problem employee."

**DISCUSSION QUESTIONS**

1. In what specific ways might a new supervisor build sufficient personal confidence to deal with a problem employee on a one-on-one basis?

2.  Assuming that the supervisor is a skillful counselor, would you give counseling a fifty-fifty chance to convert a problem employee into a superior one? Defend your answer.

3.  If a problem employee resigns voluntarily between corrective counseling sessions 1 and 2, does this mean the attempt has failed? Explain your views.

# Confrontation

### Objective

To evaluate the nature of conflicts between traditional supervisors and assertive employees.

### Problem

The relationship between Supervisor Joe and Mrs. R has deteriorated. Mrs. R is hostile, taking pot shots at Joe in conversations with co-workers, openly confronting him in staff meetings, and generally being disruptive. The situation is hurting the productivity of the department and rendering Joe ineffective. For readers not involved in role-playing, please study and evaluate the conflict between Supervisor Joe and Mrs. R as stated below.

### Players

Supervisor Joe and Mrs. R.

### Procedure

The players read their own roles (below) over and over until they are deeply into the characterization. Neither party is to communicate with the other. Mrs. R is to enter Joe's office determined to come out ahead; Joe is equally determined to resolve the problem to his satisfaction. After a ten-minute confrontation—no holds barred—both individuals are to relax and read each other's roles.

### Postgame Discussion

Discuss the nature of such conflicts and the possibility of dissipating them through the interview process. What might Joe have done to eliminate the problem in the first place? Is Mrs. R justified in her assertiveness?

### Role of Supervisor Joe

You are disturbed by Mrs. R's hostility. You recognize that she is highly capable and a high producer. You know that she has two children to raise alone. You recognize that she may become a supervisor eventually, but first you feel she should "pay her dues" as you did. You resent the fact that she is not playing by traditional rules, that she is criticizing you before your superiors and showing disrespect for you and your position among co-workers. You recall a constructive talk with her sixty days ago when you stated you would give her the training she needs to become a supervisor. You feel you have done this. You do not feel her impatience is justified. In the next few minutes you intend to listen carefully and keep an open mind, but under no circumstances will you bend your discipline line. You would be happy if Mrs. R moved to another firm.

### Role of Mrs. R

You feel your assertiveness is justified because Joe has you boxed in. He refuses to recommend you for a higher position outside his department. He doesn't appreciate your high productivity and generally fails to understand you. You recall a meeting sixty days ago when he promised to help you win a promotion to supervisor in another department. He has not fulfilled this promise. He seems to feel you should "pay a price" to him before he will go to bat for you. You have no intention of being subservient. Since you have an outstanding record within the department, you feel that any pressure you put on Joe is justified. As you enter his office, you intend to listen and keep an open mind, but if Joe doesn't handle things to your satisfaction, you intend to resign on the spot.

# STAFFING

*If you incorporate the suggestions of this chapter into your style, you will make fewer personnel mistakes and thus create a more cohesive and productive operation.*

The first employee Virginia hired on her own almost caused her to lose her own job. The story is familiar to experienced personnel directors. Without any background in interviewing, Virginia selected an individual with a persuasive personality but, also, with built-in psychological problems. Further investigation would have revealed that the applicant had been a problem employee in all of her previous jobs. Virginia lived with the situation for six months. Finally—after the human conflicts created had rendered her so ineffective her job was on the line—the individual resigned on a voluntary basis. Inexperience had caused Virginia to hire a problem rather than solve one.

As a new supervisor, you may or may not be deeply involved in the staffing process. Some supervisors have complete control over who is hired or transferred into their departments; others are assigned new employees from a personnel department with little or no say in the matter. The more your role as a supervisor involves you in the staffing process, the more important this chapter will be to you.

**Employee Turnover**

In some respects, the lower the personnel turnover in a department the better. Employee stability and high productivity often go together. But frequent personnel turnover is a fact of life. No matter how effective you become as a supervisor, now and then a key employee will shock you with a resignation. Causes range from pregnancies, to reassignment of spouses, to major career changes. On occasion, a promotion that is good for the firm will create a problem for the supervisor.

Mary was pleased management had selected Carla to supervise a newly created department. It was a high compliment to Mary who had trained Carla as her assistant. But the decision would mean screening, employing, and training a replacement. Other factors were involved. Which of her current staff could best fill Carla's shoes? Would this be a good time to reorganize the entire department? How could she turn the vacancy into an advantage?

Personnel changes present major challenges to all supervisors—challenges that must be approached with sound planning and vision.

**The Staffing Process**

Staffing includes much more than simply filling a vacancy. It also involves determining longterm personnel needs, orientation and training, transfers and reassignment, rotation, performance evaluation, and terminations. The moment a vacancy or personnel change is in the offing, experienced supervisors ask themselves these questions.

- Is the function performed by the employee leaving absolutely necessary?
- Could the tasks be divided among other employees?
- What skills are missing among the staff?
- What kind of a new person will contribute to greater productivity?
- Is someone being trained to eventually take my job as supervisor?

The goal of every supervisor should be to hire, develop, and maintain the most cohesive and productive staff possible. It is not a goal easily reached.

**Preparation for the Interview**

It is impossible to hire the best available applicant for a given job unless the skills and duties required are known ahead of time. If a printed job description is available, it should be carefully reviewed and brought up-to-date. If not, the competencies required should be written out by the supervisor. Only with such data at hand can the best match between applicants and job be achieved. Here are four additional tips.

Tip 1: Sex, race, age, or handicaps cannot play a part in the selection process. You seek the best qualified person for the job that is open. If the best qualified person happens to be different from those already in the department, she or he should still be hired.

Tip 2: The practice of first come first hired should be avoided. You can't find the best applicant without taking the time to discover what the market has to offer.

Tip 3: Screening written applications and interviewing should be done studiously. The more one rushes the process, the more subjective one becomes—and the more mistakes are made.

Tip 4: As an interview approaches, review the competencies you seek in an applicant (a competency is a skill that can be observed or measured); have a list of questions you intend to ask; know what information you need to provide applicant regarding the organization and the job—both advantages and disadvantages; and have a pad available upon which to take notes.

Interviewing a prospective new employee is a form of counseling, and the 5 R's outlined in Chapter 7 apply. Generally speaking, it is a good idea to follow these additional steps.

**Interviewing Techniques**

Step 1: Put the applicant at ease so that you can get the most reliable reactions.

Step 2: Encourage the applicant to talk through appropriate questions so you will learn about her or his potential to contribute to your department.

Step 3: Provide the applicant with an opportunity to ask questions.

Step 4: Verify the data on application form, especially that which pertains to training and skills.

Listed below are some typical questions that interviewers often ask job-seekers. Their purpose is to generate a dialogue so that a decision can be based on as much information as possible.

**Interview Questions**

- Why do you want to work here?
- What are your skill levels?
- What can you contribute?
- Why should we hire you?
- Why did you leave your last job?
- Do you have any weaknesses?
- Tell me about yourself.

Care should be taken to ask the same questions of all applicants so that each individual is given the same opportunity to communicate and, from your point of view, more objective comparisons can be made. Questions of a highly personal nature or those that will embarrass or confuse the applicant should not be used.

Employment interviews are normally divided into two different approaches. One is a guided pattern (directive); the other is less structured or unguided (non-directive). For an inexperienced interviewer, a guided pattern is often best. For example, a novice might consider using the JOB QUALIFICATION CHECK LIST printed below. The fictitious word CASSI is designed as a device to help the supervisor remember to rate all five categories in each interview.

---

### JOB QUALIFICATION CHECK LIST

| | | YES | NO |
|---|---|---|---|
| C | COOPERATIVENESS (Will the applicant make an effort to work well with the staff?) | _____ | _____ |
| A | ATTITUDE (Does the applicant have a good work attitude? Does he or she really want to produce?) | _____ | _____ |
| S | SKILLS (Does this person have all the specific skills to match the job opening?) | _____ | _____ |
| S | STABILITY (Is the applicant seeking a permanent or interim job?) | _____ | _____ |
| I | INTEREST (Has the applicant expressed high interest in the job?) | _____ | _____ |

---

Although no system is perfect, any guided pattern has the advantage of providing, at least, some objectivity. Of course, the interviewer must ask the right questions so that the above characteristics surface.

**Ending The Interview**

It is important to terminate the interview in a friendly manner without making a false commitment. A suitable closing comment might be: "We will make a decision this Friday. If you do not hear from us by next Monday, we still appreciate your interest in our organization and we will keep your application on file."

Even under ideal circumstances, a final choice is difficult to make. It is usually advisable to talk to a superior—especially if two or more candidates appear to be equally qualified.

All of the time and energy devoted to finding the best available candidate can go down the drain if the newcomer is not made a full member of the team. Chapter 11 (Supervisors Are Also Instructors) provides suggestions in accomplishing this goal. The checklist below can, also, be helpful.

**Orientation And Training**

### ORIENTATION CHECKLIST

☐ See that the new member is introduced personally to all members of the staff.

☐ Check out the use of any equipment the new employee will operate.

☐ Assign a regular employee as a sponsor to answer questions and help the new employee with adjustment.

☐ Make sure basic department rules and company policies are understood.

☐ List and discuss specific responsibilities.

☐ Follow up at the end of first day or shift to see if there are questions to be answered or adjustments to be made.

A supervisor should monitor the progress of a new employee until she or he has become a relaxed, full partner in the team and is making satisfactory progress toward maximum personal productivity. If additional training or counseling is required to reach this goal, it should be done quickly. With help, most new employees can make a complete adjustment within a period of one week.

Moving staff members into different roles for both training and motivational purposes is an excellent practice and can measurably improve departmental productivity. Sometimes the employment of a new staff member precipitates such action. Even without personnel turnover, rotating employees from job to job is a good idea in many work environments. Employees who are allowed to stay in the same job too long often fall into a low productivity rut. When given a new challenge their attitudes improve, and they make a bigger contribution. Frequently a simple job exchange can help both employees because the more experience one obtains the better prepared one becomes for future advancements—including that of supervision. In rotating or shifting employees, the following rules might apply.

**Staff Shifting And Rotation**

Rule 1: Discuss proposed changes ahead of time with all parties involved.

Rule 2: Avoid forcing new assignments, especially if the individual is insecure about having the ability to perform in the proposed role.

Rule 3: If necessary, provide additional training.

Rule 4: Give all staff members a fair chance.

Rule 5: Avoid changes unless beneficial to both employees and the department as a whole.

Rule 6: Compliment those who make adjustments gracefully.

Advanced planning accompanied by personal counseling is the key to staff shifting and rotation. Spur of the moment decisions can often do more harm than good.

Transfers   When a supervisor senses that he or she has a problem employee, the first thing that often comes to mind is a transfer to another department within the same firm. In exceptional cases—when there is an irreconcilable conflict between a supervisor and employee—such an in-house transfer may be feasible. Perhaps it will give the individual a new, fresh opportunity; perhaps she or he will be happier under a different management style. But to initiate a transfer as a ploy to get rid of a problem employee that you know will give the next supervisor a similar problem is not professional. If the request comes from a non-problem employee, it is another matter. It is possible, for example, that sometime in the future an employee of yours will ask for a transfer so that she or he will be free from your style of supervision. If this happens, do not take it personally. You cannot be expected to have the kind of style that will please everyone. In such cases, a transfer might be advantageous to all parties involved.

Justifying A   You will hear certain supervisors complaining about departmental work
Larger Staff   loads.

- "There is no way to catch up around here."
- "The more we do the more they pile it on."
- "Too much work—too few people."

Sometimes such complaints are justified. Often they are not. Only when all employees—and the supervisor—are living close to their productivity potentials, and the work load continues to increase, should a supervisor take an overload problem to his or her superior. In doing so, the following suggestions are made.

- Demonstrate your overload position with facts. Quote comparative labor cost figures with a similar operation.
- Compare today's heavier work load with that of past periods in an objective manner.
- If you can't justify a full-time, consider a part-time employee.

Whenever a supervisor seeks to increase her or his staff, management will automatically pry into the operation with a sharp eye. Only when such scrutiny produces a well-run department is such a request given serious consideration.

Supervisors who work for large organizations that have professional personnel and human resource departments have a big advantage when it comes to staffing. Most of the work—recruiting, testing, interviewing, orientation, training, terminating—is done for them by professionals. In some cases, all the supervisors need do is accept or reject a possible staff member sent to them for consideration.

**Supervisors' Relationship With Personnel Department**

It is important, however, that the supervisor do everything possible to maintain good relationships with these personnel experts. This could include:

1.  Informing personnel on the exact or changing skills and competencies you need for maximum productivity.

2.  Accepting the fact that most personnel departments do their best to attract the most qualified applicants. (Personnel people cannot change market conditions.)

3.  Abiding by Equal Opportunity Laws and other legal restrictions in dealing with employees.

4.  Paying compliments to personnel people when they are responsible for getting the right applicant to you for consideration.

When it comes to staffing problems, a supervisor's best friend is often a professional in the personnel department. Such individuals deserve, and should receive, V.I.P. treatment.

**DISCUSSION QUESTIONS**

1.  Are the advantages of job rotation within most departments worth the effort? If so, why do the majority of supervisors avoid the process?

2.  If you were a supervisor for an organization that assigned new employees to your department without giving you the opportunity to interview or reject applicants, would you make an attempt to change the procedure? If so, how would you go about doing it?

3.  In addition to reviewing the material in this chapter, what might a supervisor do to obtain additional information and insights into staffing problems and interviewing techniques?

# QUALIFICATIONS

You manage a highly successful fast food operation in a small, isolated community. Last week you received an award at an employer banquet sponsored by the local high school. The citation recognized your contribution to the training of local youth. You are proud to have it hanging in your office.

Yesterday, you interviewed five applicants for a part-time position as counter-girl. The qualifications are speed and accuracy with numbers, agility in counting change quickly, and a positive attitude with customers. The best qualified applicant was obviously an experienced sixty-year old lady, but you passed her up because you felt she would not work well with high school students and, as a result, would not last long.

Are you and the company you work for vulnerable to an age discrimination complaint? Defend your answer.

# Delegate More—Worry Less

*When you have completed this chapter, you should be able to (1) write out five reasons why supervisors don't delegate responsibilities and duties often enough, (2) describe the conditions under which a supervisor should delegate more, and (3) write out in specific terms how to do it.*

"For Pete's sake, Harry, turn some of that stuff over to your employees and relax a little."

"Good grief, Sally, it's ridiculous for you to kill yourself doing such routine work when you have nine people in your department who need the experience."

"Come off it, Frank. You'd have plenty of time for more important things if you'd delegate some of those jobs you shouldn't be doing in the first place."

Sound familiar? Yes, it's easy to tell others to delegate and it's true that most supervisors should delegate more, but most of us have to learn the lesson the hard way. Take Dee as an example.

Dee was a new, young, capable, and highly enthusiastic manager. She had five full-time and three part-time employees. Despite advice from all sides, she could not learn to assign responsible work to others. Instead of delegating more, she simply pushed herself harder. Dee was so eager to be a successful supervisor that she was blind to what was happening. One of her best friends told her to manage more and do less. Her boss took her aside and gave her a heart-to-heart talk about the problem, but with little success.

Then one afternoon Dee passed out on the job and was taken by ambulance to a local hospital. The diagnosis was complete exhaustion. Dee hadn't received the message from her friends or boss, but she heard it loud and clear from her doctor. He put it very simply: either she must learn to delegate or she could forget about being a supervisor.

Delegating can, of course, mean many things to many people, but primarily it involves turning important work over to someone else. It means giving others the authority to do an assignment, with expected results mutually understood, but keeping the reponsibility yourself. It means having sufficient faith in others to let them do important work for you.

Personnel directors for large organizations are in an excellent position to analyze and compare how supervisors delegate. Here are three penetrating comments.

"When it comes to delegating, most inexperienced supervisors make two big mistakes: (1) they fail to do it skillfully and (2) they fail to delegate enough. Delegation of duties is difficult to put into actual practice."

"The problem with delegating is that most supervisors know they *should* do it and most *think* they do it, but few *really* do it and those who do often go about it awkwardly."

"Some supervisors never sense the extent to which delegating can help their careers or realize the degree of skill it takes to do it properly."

Delegating responsibilities and duties to others is a must. Unless you learn to do it often and skillfully, your future as a manager may be seriously limited.

## Failure to Delegate

Why do some supervisors fail to delegate as much as they should? There are four basic reasons, all psychological in nature.

### No Faith in Subordinates

Many supervisors do not see enough potential for success in the people who work for them and, as a result, never give their employees important and difficult assignments. Sometimes this happens because the supervisor has been burned in the past by poor performance; sometimes it is caused by unrealistic standards set by the supervisor. Most supervisors, however, simply lack confidence in the performance possibilities of employees. Unfortunately, this very lack of confidence often results in poor performance when the supervisor is forced to delegate. To delegate successfully, you must have confidence in the results you anticipate and transmit this feeling to the employee.

Every time you delegate important work to others, you risk failure and possible criticism from your superiors. You lay your personal reputation on the line. That's as it should be. If you are not sufficiently secure in your job and with your company to take a few failures, then you shouldn't be a supervisor in the first place. Fear is a powerful emotion that can tie you up in knots and cause you to be too cautious. You must conquer such fears before you can delegate freely and effectively. **Fear of Superiors**

Some supervisors with a strong need for ego-fulfillment try to do all the important work themselves so they will receive personal credit from their superiors. In taking this narrow perspective, they fail to see that by relinquishing personal credit to their employees they can (through motivation of individuals) increase productivity which, in turn, will improve the reputation of the department. It is shortsighted for a supervisor to want personal credit when departmental success will ultimately be more beneficial. **Desire for Personal Credit**

Many supervisors are also shortsighted about time. They refuse to take time to delegate a responsibility today to free themselves for more important work next week. Time is the supervisor's most important commodity. If you refuse to delegate because doing it properly takes too much time, you are guilty of very poor planning. Skillful delegating saves time. **Misjudgment of Time**

When should the supervisor delegate? You might wait forever for the perfect time to delegate, but some delegation should take place under the following conditions. **When and How to Delegate**

1. When you need more time for work that only you can do, especially planning responsibilities that will contribute more to departmental productivity than the job being delegated.
2. When delegating will help involve employees, improve their morale, and cause them to work closer to their potentials.
3. When it will not show undue favoritism or seriously damage relationships with other employees.
4. When you are willing to take the time and effort to do a skillful job of delegating.

5. When you are under pressure and must get rid of some responsibilities in order to protect your physical and mental health.

How can you delegate skillfully? Everyone agrees that surfing, skydiving, and water-skiing take skill, but few people will acknowledge that the same is true of delegating. Yet delegating has its own special procedures. If you follow the five steps below, you will greatly improve your skill in delegating.

**Select the Task Carefully**

Make up a priority list of assignments you might delegate. For a job to qualify for this list, it should be taking too much of your time, should be rather low in responsibility compared to your other duties, and should be good for your employees to do. Once you have your list, start from the top and delegate one task at a time. Try to spread them out over all your employees until you sense you are reaching a saturation point.

**Select the Person Carefully**

Consider all factors involved before selecting the person to whom you will give a specified task. Which employees have too much or too little work to do? Is there an individual who needs a special challenge? Will the individual you select accept it with enthusiasm? Does the person have the talent to execute it well? How will co-workers react? Will it increase departmental productivity? Obviously, you must know your employees well if assignments are to fit the special needs and talents of each.

**Prepare All Individuals for Change**

Since sudden unannounced changes can disturb people and hurt productivity, announce your decision carefully in order to protect your relationships with all employees and to give the employee receiving the assignment all possible assistance. In most cases a group announcement is best so that everyone is informed, misunderstandings are eliminated, and there is an opportunity to ask questions. In delegating, you must be concerned with the feelings of all employees and not just those of the person to whom you are delegating.

**Turn Over the Assignment**

Consider the following steps outlined below in turning over new responsibilities to an employee:

1. Meet in private where you will not be interrupted.
2. Allocate sufficient time to delegate carefully and thoroughly.
3. Go over the new job step by step. Illustrate whenever possible.
4. Ask the employee for a verbal feedback on all details presented to eliminate future misunderstandings.
5. Give employee an opportunity to ask questions.
6. Compliment the employee on previous work and transmit confidence in the way she or he will perform the new responsibility.

Soon after delegating, make yourself available to answer further questions and provide additional training. Overheard questions similar to these often facilitate communications.

How are you doing on the new equipment?
How do you feel now about your new assignment?
Do you need any help I have not provided?
Do you have any suggestions for me or other employees?

To delegate without a follow-up is to ask for trouble and disappointment. You can delegate authority, but not your responsibility. You must know how things are going. You must satisfy yourself.

If you learn to delegate frequently and skillfully, you'll eventually worry less, feel less pressured, have more time to plan and organize, build better relationships with your employees, and motivate greater productivity in your department.

**DISCUSSION QUESTIONS**

1. Draw up a profile of an individual who, because of certain personality traits, might not be able to delegate and therefore should not be a supervisor.

2. Would most employees be happier and produce more if they were given more responsibilities by their managers? Why or why not?

3. Why do so many supervisors use the lack of time as an excuse for not delegating? How would you convince such a person that spending time now can save time later?

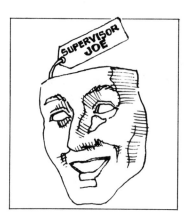

# Delegation

### Objective

To provide simulated practice in delegating.

### Problem

Supervisor Joe has taken a close look at himself and his department and has decided that he *must* delegate more of his duties to his employees for the following reasons: (1) He has been working fifty hours a week instead of forty. (2) The pressure of trying to get everything done has put him on edge with some of the staff. (3) He has not been sleeping well because of worry. Last night he spent three hours formulating the following list of responsibilities he might delegate to his five employees.

1. *A weekly report that takes fifty minutes to prepare.* This report could easily be delegated to Mrs. R, but it would reveal certain departmental figures that have not been revealed to employees in the past. There is nothing secret about the data, but Joe feels he might lose control if everybody knows what goes on.

2. *A weekly job that Joe has always enjoyed doing.* Mrs. Q would love to do the job (she would probably do it better than Joe), but Joe wants to keep it because it keeps him closer to his employees and facilitates communication. This job usually takes about one hour.

3. *A very routine weekly stock or supply room count that takes an hour and a half.* Joe has delegated this job before, but he always winds up taking it back because the grumbling from the employee disturbs him more than doing the job himself. Besides, sometimes the count is wrong, and he ends up doing the job himself anyway.

4. *A very short (fifteen-minute) telephone call every day at 4:00 p.m. to send some data to the computer center.* Joe has refused to delegate this

because if it is not done accurately he will be reprimanded by Mr. Big. Mr. K would be able to do the job and not be overloaded.

5. *A daily (ten-minute) delivery job of a special report to top management.* Joe has kept this to do himself because it gives him a chance to have a cup of coffee and he can play a little politics with middle (and sometimes top) management executives.

6. *A special routine meeting each month, which many supervisors already delegate to a subordinate.* It would be excellent training for Mr. G to have this assignment. Joe has kept it to himself, however, because he is afraid that something will happen at the meeting that he won't know about.

## Players

No role assignments. All participants play themselves. Those readers not involved in group role playing are encouraged to prioritize the six activities based upon the principles discussed in the chapter.

## Procedure

Players number off from one to five to form five small groups, with each number 1 as a group leader. Each group is to find a quiet location where they can discuss Joe's list of six tasks that could be delegated. Which should be delegated first? Which last? Each group should assign a priority number from one to six to each possibility. The leader of each group should try to get complete agreement on the allocation of priority numbers within a fifteen-minute period. The following factors should be taken into consideration: Try to (1) save Joe as much time as possible, (2) relieve him of menial tasks, (3) improve departmental productivity, (4) train others for future supervisory roles, and (5) improve Joe's image as a supervisor. Once each group has completed its priority list, results should be recorded on a master schedule on the blackboard.

MASTER SCHEDULE

| Responsibility | Grp. 1 | Grp. 2 | Grp. 3 | Grp. 4 | Grp. 5 | Grp. 6 | Class Choice |
|---|---|---|---|---|---|---|---|
| 1. Weekly Report | | | | | | | |
| 2. Fun Job | | | | | | | |
| 3. Stock Count | | | | | | | |
| 4. Telephone Call | | | | | | | |

5. Delivery Job   ———————————————————

6. Special Meeting   ———————————————————

After each group has recorded its choice, the points should be added horizontally and the total put in the last column under class choice. The lower the number, the higher priority given by the class. Any group that matches the class choice is a winner.

**Postgame Discussion**

Should Joe delegate all six possibilities? Which, if any, should he keep to himself? What other factors should he take into consideration?

# Supervisors Are Also Instructors

*If you learn and apply the four-step teaching formula presented in this chapter, you will earn the respect that comes from being an excellent on-the-job instructor.*

Employees usually take pride in learning a difficult new skill. When you make this learning possible, you earn their respect and build enduring, productive, relationships. As a supervisor, you have daily opportunities to provide instruction.

The supervisor is frequently the only person who teaches the many skills that new employees need to learn: how to operate machines, complete forms, understand procedures, work skillfully with difficult customers or patients, complete reports, maintain equipment, and so on,

**105**

down a long list. Permanent employees need to learn how to operate new generations of equipment, follow changing procedures, and perform tasks more effectively. On-the-job training never stops.

**How to Teach by Not Teaching**

You can become an outstanding on-the-job instructor without employing any of the formal methods we usually associate with the traditional classroom teacher. All supervisors are models, and to a surprising extent your employees will adjust their behavior to the model you set. They will learn a great deal from you without your knowing it. But they also need specific help from you, and you want to provide this help in your own style without being tabbed as a ''teacher.'' Instead of saying to a new employee, ''Let me teach you how to do this,'' it might be better to say, ''Let's figure out how you can do this quickly, comfortably, and correctly.'' Instead of saying to a regular employee, ''Let me teach you to do it right the first time,'' it might be better to say, ''Let me show you how I do this, and then you can figure out the best way for you to do it.'' It is one thing to be an effective classroom teacher—it is something else to be an effective on-the-job instructor.

**Your Attitude Toward Teaching**

What is your personal *attitude* toward sharing your knowledge with employees? Are you willing to set aside enough time to do it professionally? Do you desire to build a good reputation as a patient, caring instructor? *Are you more like Marvin or Max?*

Marvin accepts a new employee where she or he is as far as experience and ability to learn is concerned. When assuming his teaching role, he is patient, positive, and thorough even if the learner is slow to catch on. As a result, Marvin develops a cohesive, productive, and loyal staff. His patient teaching attitude is admired and respected.

Max consistently complains that new employees should have learned more in school. He shows little patience in teaching others. As a result, his staff makes more mistakes and personnel turnover is high. New workers are often forced to go to co-workers for help they need. Max's negative attitude toward teaching others creates problems instead of solving them.

**The Four-Step Process**

For years professional instructors have followed the four-step teaching process that is best used in practical on-the-job situations. You may wish to view this process as a baseball game in that you have four bases to cover before you can score. In other words, you (the instructor) will take the employee (learner) around four bases, one at a time. What follows will show you the moves you should make, the dangers you face, and the signals you should follow.

Prepare the Worker

Because it's difficult to learn until one is psychologically and emotionally ready, your first responsibility is to help the new employee prepare for what you will teach. There are four steps to follow in doing this.

*Put the learner at ease.*    Give the employee time to adjust to you as a person before you move into teaching the job itself. Find out a little more about the employee, make small talk, and try to put the person at ease. A worker who fears you cannot learn well from you, so make the effort to establish a relaxed learning climate. It's time well spent.

*State the job you are going to teach and find out what the employee already knows about it.*    Do not waste time (or insult the employee) by teaching something he or she already knows. You may discover a quick review is all that is necessary.

*Motivate the person to learn the job.*    Give the worker some reason to learn. You might suggest that it could help the individual earn the respect of others, or you might talk about the personal satisfaction and pride that can come from learning something new. Make it sound exciting. Your job as a teacher will be much easier if the worker wants to learn.

*Place the worker in the correct learning position.*    Just as a baseball player must have the right stance to hit the ball, it might be best for the worker to be on your left hand instead of your right side or to stand instead of sit. Determine the best physical position for the learner in each job you teach and be certain he or she is located properly before you start. Attention to this factor will make the job easier for both parties.

Preparing the worker is comparable to reaching first base, and now you are ready to try for second. The following three steps will take you there with little difficulty.

**Present Operation**

*Describe, illustrate, and demonstrate one important step in a task at a time.*    Do not give so much information at once that the learner becomes confused. This is not easy to do, because you know the job so well that it's hard for you to remember how long it took you to learn it.

Tell the worker how to do the job, speaking clearly and slowly. Use simple words. If you must use a technical term, be sure to explain what you mean.

Whenever possible, follow up with an illustration. Take out your pencil and sketch the process—it need not be a work of art to convey the message. Show the learner by actually performing the job yourself, one step at a time. Be sure that you perform in slow motion so that your actions are easily observed.

*Stress each key point.*    Determine and then stress the one key point in each separate step of the operation as you go through the process. This will help the learner recall each step later by remembering the key points and the process will thereby become easier. When there are more than five steps to a given job, this procedure becomes increasingly important.

*Instruct clearly, completely, and patiently but don't give the worker more than can be mastered.* The greatest error that most supervisors commit is trying to teach too much too fast. They overestimate their teaching abilities and the employee's learning ability. If you try to teach too much at one time, you will only confuse the learner, and you'll have to start over. Break the total job into separate steps and present them in sequence. Do not start the second step until the first has been mastered. If necessary, permit a lapse of time between steps. Focus on teaching the material thoroughly, even though time is at a premium.

**Supervise a Trial Performance**
Give the new worker an immediate opportunity to actually do the job on a trial basis following this three-step procedure.

*Have the learner do the job so that you can correct errors quickly.* Few new workers perform jobs perfectly the first time, and the only way to spot errors is to have the worker try out the process under your direction. Of course, errors should be pointed out and corrected quickly without showing impatience.

*Have the employee explain the key points about the job.* It is important that the key points learned in the second step be repeated verbally by the learner during the first performance. Explaining each one makes it easier to remember.

*Make sure the worker understands.* It is vital that the learner understand why it is best to do a job in a certain way and why the job is important to the total efficiency of the department. Give the employee the opportunity to ask questions.

The idea of this third step is to continue until *you* know the learner knows. If necessary, continue the dry runs until the skill is mastered.

**Follow Up the Performance**
Sometimes the most difficult step of all is the follow-up. To guarantee long-term performance at high levels, try the following steps.

*Tell the worker where to go for help.* If you are not easily accessible to the new worker, find a sponsor to help the employee achieve and keep a high level of productivity. In short, appoint a co-worker who will be compatible with the new employee and willing to help when needed.

*Check frequently to see if all is going well.* Take time to check with the worker as well as the sponsor. Nothing can replace your own interest during the employee's first critical days of learning.

*Taper off coaching so that the worker doesn't feel oversupervised.* After a certain point the employee deserves the satisfaction and freedom of going it alone. This will provide the confidence needed to assume further responsibility at a later date. Oversupervising can destroy initiative. Pull away when your job performance standards have been met.

If you successfully follow these steps, you will be an excellent teacher and supervisor. The new worker will know how to do the job, will do it right the first time, and will have the confidence to be a long-term, productive member of your department. You will have begun to establish a solid relationship with the new worker.

If you have tried the four basic steps and still feel that you have failed in your efforts to train a new employee, the cause may be one or more of the following three errors.

1. *Failure to devote enough time to teaching.* You must allow sufficient time to do the teaching job properly, even if it means putting aside some of your other responsibilities temporarily. It won't be easy to do, but the long-range productivity of your workers will prove that you have spent your time well.

2. *Failure to follow the system step by step.* The system provided in this chapter takes time but it works. If you skip a step, the system will break down and you'll fail.

3. *Failure to show enough patience with the slow learner.* Few new workers will be as smart as you would like them to be. Some may learn more slowly then employees you have trained in the past. When you must teach a slow learner to do a job, you must slow your own pace or the results will be most disappointing. Cover each of the four bases with special patience and consideration even if it means taking twice as much time as you had devoted in the past. Keep in mind that slow learners can become excellent producers once they master the job, so the extra time you devote will not be wasted.

**Delegating Training Responsibilities**

Professional educators frequently admit that the best way to learn to do something well is to teach it. There are times when you may wish to delegate the training of a new employee to a regular employee who fully understands and practices the four-step process effectively. By delegating you will give recognition to the regular employee, provide excellent training to the new employee, and save yourself time. It may be wise, however, for you to retain the follow-up responsibility to make certain the employee you selected as a sponsor does the job correctly.

**Group Instruction**

As a supervisor you may be invited to make a presentation to other supervisors and your superiors. You can prepare for the event by making one or more group presentations to your own employees. Follow the same basic steps you use in individual instruction. That is, prepare the group (audience), present the new material (knowledge), gain involvement through questions, and summarize (follow through) by repeating the goal of the meeting.

As you follow these basic principles, you might also consider the following:

1. The more visual aids you prepare in advance, the more confidence you will have in your presentation and the more effective you will be.
2. Generally speaking, lecturing is the least effective teaching method, so strive for as much group interaction as possible.
3. Cover your subject carefully but remember it is better to take too little time than too much.

Training never stops. As long as you must cope with an ever-increasing number of changes, you must learn new teaching techniques and pass them on to those who work with you. Everyone, including your superiors, finds it stressful to keep up with changes both in the environment in general and within the organization in particular. You will need to train yourself to deal with the impact of change, which means you will need to learn new ways to perform responsibilities. The greater the changes, the more you must learn; the more you learn, the more time you must spend instructing others.

Changes manifest themselves in different ways—new procedures, new techniques, new generations of equipment, new skills, and new ways of dealing with problems. As changes occur, you should constantly search for new ideas and procedures to put into your own personal ''knowledge bag.'' You should continue to educate yourself through both self-instruction and formal course programs. When you learn something that will improve the productivity of your department, you should pass it on, using the four-step method, to your staff.

They depend upon you to keep them informed.

**DISCUSSION QUESTIONS**

1. Assume that you are going to start taking skydiving lessons tomorrow. Would you want your instructor to use the four-step system?

2. From your experience as a nonsupervisor (learner), do you feel supervisors, generally speaking, are good instructors? Cite examples to support your view.

3. How can a supervisor train himself or herself to spend sufficient time on quality instruction that will earn respect from employees? Be specific.

# Training

Mr. Big has become increasingly disturbed over high personnel turnover, low productivity, and the increasing number of mistakes made by new employees in all of the departments under his management. As a result, he has designed a new orientation plan based upon the premise that the quality of on-the-job training has not been up to standard. The supervisor will be totally responsible for the implementation and success of orientation.

The new plan specifies:

(1) The four-step teaching method is mandated.
(2) At the end of two weeks, the new employee and his or her supervisor will meet in Mr. Big's office for an evaluation and progress report.
(3) Those supervisors who receive high marks from a new employee indicating that on-the-job learning has been at a high level will receive, as a reward, a one-time-only three-day weekend.

How do you respond to this plan? Do you feel the supervisor has been given a proper role in the plan? Will it reduce turnover, increase productivity, and curtail mistakes? What negative side effects might it generate? Is the plan too ambitious? Would Mr. Big have time to follow through on all evaluations?

Is Mr. Big being too heavy-handed in his approach?

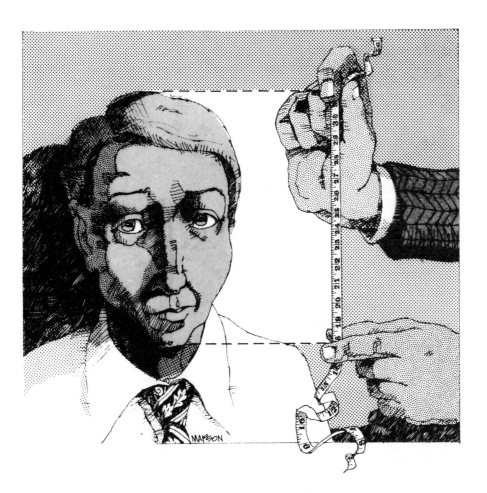

# The Formal Appraisal

*After you read and apply the techniques described in this chapter, one of the following should occur: (1) if you have already done a formal appraisal, your technique should improve noticeably the next time, or (2) if you have never done a formal appraisal, you should be able to do a better than average job the first time.*

In most sizable organizations supervisors appraise each individual in their departments every six months or once a year. If you have been on the receiving end of such an appraisal, you probably still remember the supervisor, the printed instrument, the interview, and the results. The purpose of this chapter is to prepare you to administer such evaluations for the first time—or to help you improve upon the way you have handled them in the past.

Appraisals give you an opportunity to improve your counseling techniques. They permit you to apply the Five R's of Counseling you learned

**113**

in Chapter 7. As such, they should be viewed as a positive experience—something you can learn to do well now that will stand you in good stead as you move into higher management roles.

**Appraisal Instruments**

You cannot accomplish an appraisal without using a form or rating sheet which, after the interview is over, becomes a permanent record. There are almost as many different appraisal instruments as there are organizations that use them. Few, if any, fully satisfy the people who designed them or the managers who use them. Almost any form, however, can be used effectively if the supervisor's attitude toward it is positive.

Two examples of appraisal instruments are shown on pages 115–119.

**Appraisals and M.B.O.**

There is an important relationship between formal appraisals and Management by Objectives philosophies. For example, your superior (evaluating you as a supervisor) might tie your appraisal to the success you have had in reaching the objectives you submitted at an earlier time. If you have made excellent progress towards the goals approved earlier, chances are good you will receive a positive report. Other factors that may be considered include human relations skills, dependability, and the ability to handle problem employees.

In a sense, a formal appraisal is a form of accountability. You are asked to account for your past performance based upon certain standards that are included on the rating sheet. In a majority of organizations salary increases, bonuses, and other forms of compensation are tied to performance rating. Results are therefore critical to those being appraised.

**Appraisals and Career Planning**

It is inevitable and fortuitous that going through the evaluation process frequently causes employees to review their own career progress or master plans. More than anything else an appraisal tells you "how you are doing" and whether or not you should make adjustments to your long-term career path. It is a time of self-evaluation.

As a front-line supervisor, you will want to tie your appraisals into the future planning of your employees. If they receive weak appraisals, what can they do to make improvements before the next period arrives? What self-improvement projects might they undertake to eliminate deficiencies?

Mrs. Petronzio was the director of a convalescent home with a staff of thirty-six. This year, for the first time, she was required by new management to do appraisals on all employees. She viewed the new responsibility as a challenge that could increase staff productivity, and spent considerable time reading up on techniques and getting acquainted with the form.

Her first appraisal was with Maisie, a vocational nurse, who was highly dependable and capable of taking over any position that did not require the presence of a registered nurse. Mrs. Petronzio rated Maisie excellent in every

## EVALUATION OF WORK PERFORMANCE

QUANTITY
of Individual's Work

| LOW | LESS THAN ACCEPTABLE | COMPLETELY ACCEPTABLE | MORE THAN ACCEPTABLE | HIGH |
|---|---|---|---|---|

SUPPORTING COMMENTS: _____

_____

_____

_____

_____

QUALITY
of Individual's Work

| LOW | LESS THAN ACCEPTABLE | COMPLETELY ACCEPTABLE | MORE THAN ACCEPTABLE | HIGH |
|---|---|---|---|---|

SUPPORTING COMMENTS: _____

_____

_____

_____

_____

CONTRIBUTIONS
to Work Group's Performance

| LOW | LESS THAN ACCEPTABLE | COMPLETELY ACCEPTABLE | MORE THAN ACCEPTABLE | HIGH |
|---|---|---|---|---|

SUPPORTING COMMENTS: _____

_____

_____

_____

SIGNATURE OF EMPLOYEE _____ PREPARED BY _____

 **HEWLETT PACKARD**

# PERFORMANCE EVALUATION AND
# DEVELOPMENT PLAN
## general

Name: _____
                    (Emp. No.)

Date Hired: _____

Job Title: _____

Time in Present Position: _____

Date of Evaluation: _____

Division and Dept.: _____

Evaluating Manager: _____
                            (Signature)

Reviewed By: _____
                    (Next Level of Mgmt.)

---

The purpose of this evaluation is to:
1. **Set Goals.**  The manager and the employee establish mutually agreed-upon goals for future progress and development.
2. **Inform.**  The manager and the employee communicate openly and honestly about performance.
3. **Develop.**  The manager and employee identify actions the employee can take to enhance his or her development at HP.
4. **Evaluate.** The manager and the employee evaluate results based on pre-established goals and performance measures.

---

I.   **POSITION OBJECTIVES AND MAJOR RESPONSIBILITIES.** Summarize specific responsibilities of the job.

_____
_____
_____
_____
_____
_____
_____
_____
_____
_____
_____
_____

II.  **ACCOMPLISHMENTS AND/OR IMPROVEMENTS:** What specific accomplishments and/or improvements has this individual made since the last review? What progress has been made toward meeting established performance goals?

_____
_____
_____
_____
_____
_____
_____
_____
_____
_____
_____
_____
_____

9320-2944 (3/80)

Please consider the employee's demonstrated performance and mark the circle which most closely describes that performance.

EXCEPTIONAL:   Performance consistently far exceeds expectations.

VERY GOOD:   Performance consistently exceeds normal expectations and job requirements.

GOOD:   Performance consistently meets expectations and job requirements.

ACCEPTABLE:   Performance usually meets expectations and minimum requirements for the job.

UNACCEPTABLE: Performance is below the minimum acceptable level.

**WORK QUALITY:** The reliability, accuracy and neatness of work produced.

○ Exceptional     ○ Very Good     ○ Good     ○ Acceptable     ○ Unacceptable

**WORK QUANTITY:** The amount or volume of work turned out.

○ Exceptional     ○ Very Good     ○ Good     ○ Acceptable     ○ Unacceptable

**JUDGMENT:** The ability to make well-reasoned, sound decisions which affect work performance.

○ Exceptional     ○ Very Good     ○ Good     ○ Acceptable     ○ Unacceptable

**INITIATIVE:** The combination of job interest, dedication, and willingness to extend oneself to complete assigned tasks.

   ○ Exceptional     ○ Very Good     ○ Good     ○ Acceptable     ○ Unacceptable

_____

_____

_____

_____

_____

_____

**TEAMWORK:** The working relationship established with fellow employees in the working environment.

   ○ Exceptional     ○ Very Good     ○ Good     ○ Acceptable     ○ Unacceptable

_____

_____

_____

_____

_____

_____

**DEPENDABILITY:** The reliance which can be placed on an employee to persevere and carry through to completion any task assigned. This also applies to attendance and punctuality.

   ○ Exceptional     ○ Very Good     ○ Good     ○ Acceptable     ○ Unacceptable

_____

_____

_____

_____

_____

_____

**PERFORMANCE SUMMARY:** _____

_____

_____

_____

_____

_____

_____

_____

_____

_____

_____

_____

_____

_____

_____

_____

_____

_____

III. **DEVELOPMENT PLAN:** What specific action can you suggest to help the employee improve their performance? How can you, as the manager, help?

_____
_____
_____
_____
_____
_____
_____
_____
_____
_____
_____
_____
_____
_____

IV. **NEXT YEAR'S GOAL STATEMENTS:** Establish with your manager goals which may include new and better ways to carry out job responsibilities, as well as plans for personal development. Stated goals should be included as basis for next formal performance evaluation.

_____
_____
_____
_____
_____
_____
_____
_____
_____
_____

V. **EMPLOYEE COMMENTS:** Each individual evaluated is encouraged to add any comments to this review. If additional space is needed, attach a separate sheet.

_____
_____
_____
_____
_____
_____
_____
_____

I am signing this evaluation to indicate that my manager and I have had a discussion of the above comments.

_____          _____
Date                                      Employee Signature

Reproduced by permission of Hewlett-Packard, Inc.

category but cooperativeness because, in recent months, Maisie had become irritated with others in a variety of situations.

Under Mrs. Petronzio's gentle probing, Maisie admitted she was frequently upset over the poor attitudes and performance of registered nurses who were paid substantially more than she. When Mrs. Petronzio suggested that Maisie could qualify as a registered nurse with special training at a local college, she was interested. Eventually she undertook the program. Not only did Maisie receive an excellent rating in all factors the next time around but, after three years of training, she became a registered nurse— something that might not have occurred without the formal appraisal interview.

**Benefits to Management**

Who benefits from these formal performance review programs? Why are they used so often? Are they truly helpful to employees?

Management has good reason for supporting the program and insisting that all people (including themselves) be measured occasionally under a standardized procedure.

1. It's the best way to make sure that the high-production employee is identified and recognized and that the low-production employee is located and counseled.

2. Properly administered by the first-line supervisor, the system will build a stronger working relationship between the supervisor and the employee and thus help improve performance.

3. The policy produces a more objective basis for salary increases and promotions.

4. A formal system, though never perfected, will provide better and more uniform treatment of individuals by supervisors than having no system.

Management, however, is first to recognize that the key to the success of the appraisal system is its administration. This is why supervisors are being given more and more training to make the system work. (And this is why you are reading this chapter.)

**Benefits to Employees**

It's easy to see why management endorses a good appraisal system properly administered, but what about its benefits to employees? Do they really come out ahead? In the great majority of cases, the answer is *yes* for the following reasons:

1. The procedure clarifies what is expected of the employee.
2. It provides a system of recognition and prevents employees from being ignored or lost.

3. It forces the supervisor to speak up or shut up on negative matters, thus creating a more objective and open relationship with the employee.
4. The rating helps the employee know weak areas so improvements can be made.
5. It forces periodic communications between the supervisor and the employee.

These are all good reasons, but then why are rating systems so unpopular? Many employees complain every time their review period comes along, and some supervisors dread the process just as much. If the problem is so beneficial, why do supervisors and employees react in this way?

Supervisors usually take one of two positions when it comes to formal reviews. Those who choose the first position see the value in the process and turn it into a positive tool. Their employees look forward to it. Those who take the other position refuse to see the purpose and fight the process most of the way. Their employees resent the procedure as much as their supervisors do. In other words, you as the administrating official determine the success or failure of any rating system; you can look forward to every review situation or you can try to avoid it. How you handle the procedure will determine whether your employees consider it an opportunity or a disagreeable chore.

**Using a Positive Approach**

The positive approach pays off for professional supervisors because they use the merit rating system to improve productivity in their departments. They take advantage of the procedure to build better relationships with their people. They make it a vehicle to get raises and promotions for their better employees. Here are some suggestions to help you turn formal reviews into a positive rather than a negative force.

You are a supervisor, not the owner of the firm, a C.E.O., or a personnel director charged with responsibility for the program. If you spend your time complaining and trying to change the system, you won't have enough time left to make it work.

Accept the System the Way It Is

With all your responsibilities you may be tempted to back away from an honest appraisal of your people by giving them a better rating than they deserve, sometimes referred to as the error of leniency. Employees know how they perform better than you do and may lose respect for you if you are too soft or permit intimidation. Most employees want an honest evaluation and may feel shortchanged and disappointed if you don't give it to them. On the other hand, be sure to be fair. A minimal rating or a grudgingly given high mark may leave the employee

Don't Take the Easy Way Out

feeling unappreciated. When this happens, motivation to produce can drop dramatically. As you complete the rating form, try following these suggestions.

1. Remember you are appraising the employee's work, not his or her personality. Base your evaluation on objective data such as production figures, competence, attendance records, or mistakes.

2. Avoid basing your evaluation more on the potential of the employee rather than on actual performance. Evaluate what the employee contributed to the department's productivity, not what he or she is capable of contributing.

3. Base your evaluation on the employee's average performance during the period covered, not on isolated examples of extremely good or bad work. One good or bad day, week, or month shouldn't necessarily result in a corresponding high or low rating.

4. Avoid the halo effect. In other words, rather than permitting one prominent quality (good or bad) to influence your rating of other factors, include all important productivity factors.

5. Avoid the error of central tendency in which you select the middle rating on all factors. This usually happens when the supervisors are in a hurry or want to play it safe because they don't want to accept the responsibility.

The modern approach to performance appraisal differs from the traditional approach in both emphasis and content. Some of the distinguishing characteristics are: (1) The salary-wage interview is often separated from the performance improvement interview so that the salary matter does not dominate the discussion. (2) The performance appraisal is future-oriented instead of focusing on past results. (3) Emphasis is placed upon the establishment of work objectives that can be achieved by the next evaluation period, not on negative criticism about past performance. (4) The basic idea is to develop a supportive climate and improve the relationship between the supervisor and the employee through non-evaluative listening, nondirective counseling, and performance feedback.

Always Discuss the Rating Openly with Employees

Different organizations follow different procedures: (1) Some require that employees evaluate themselves first and then let the supervisor react. (2) some require the supervisor to rate the employees first and then let them react. (3) Some leave it up to the supervisor.

Regardless of the system (and there are advantages to each), you should openly discuss the rating with the employee, explaining and, if necessary, defending your position on all factors rated. Try to establish a two-way communication in which the employee has a free and fair chance to present his or her case. An employee rating without an unhurried discussion may be in compliance with the system, but it is a mockery of its purpose. Sometimes, of course, the formal appraisal results in a salary increase for the employee. When the supervisor can take this surprise into the post-appraisal counseling period, he or she has every psychological advantage.

There is no way to hurry through the formal appraisal and still have it accomplish its purpose. To rush the procedure is to destroy it. You must *make* time to do it properly.

**Give the Appraisal the Time It Deserves**

You must be sure of your ground when you rate an employee in a way that will affect the individual's future. When you must give an unsatisfactory rating, make sure you follow these steps: (1) Have all the facts at your disposal. (2) Discuss the problem with the employee. (3) Take your decision to both your manager and the personnel director. (4) Be ready to recognize an improvement in productivity if and when it happens.

**Protect Yourself on Below-Standard Ratings**

Introspective self-evaluation is the primary purpose of any appraisal program. It is not a tool to embarrass, intimidate, dispose of, annoy, or harass an employee but rather to help the employee gauge his or her progress and future with the company. Geared to the needs of the employee, the system cannot fail; geared exclusively to the needs of the organization, it becomes suspect and loses its value.

**Use the Appraisal as a Positive Tool**

Sometimes you may be so enthusiastic over an outstanding appraisal that you either make or imply a promise that you can't keep in a reasonable length of time. Nothing destroys morale more than an unkept promise. Therefore you must protect everyone by making only clear statements which cannot be misinterpreted.

**Be Careful with Promises**

Don't convey to the employee that once the regular appraisal is over, no further help or counseling will occur until the next time around. If the appraisal was positive, the employee may feel you will ignore future problems. If it was negative, he or she may feel that you won't be available for more help until the next appraisal session. Good follow-up procedures are essential to the success of the system.

**Follow Up with Compliments or Further Counseling**

There are as many appraisal systems as there are organizations, most of which seem overcomplicated with too much detail. Even so, try to go along with the system by following the instructions carefully. Follow the necessary red tape without griping. The system depends on you to make it work.

**Do the Necessary Paperwork on Time**

Take Special Pains with the First Appraisal

The first time an employee is formally appraised can be extremely important to both the individual and the organization. Take extra time to (1) explain the purpose and procedure, (2) go over the form in detail so that there are no misunderstandings, and (3) make sure the employee has an opportunity to ask questions and to feel at home with the procedure.

To fairly judge, measure, or evaluate the performance of another person is a sensitive, difficult process. Realizing that it is never easy to separate performance from personality, accept all available help to keep the procedure from backfiring and causing serious human problems. The suggestions listed above will help you stay on the right track, but they cannot remove the responsibility of the ultimate rating decision from your shoulders. You are the only one close enough to the employee to have all the necessary facts and data, who can provide the quality counseling that must accompany the process, and who can translate the theory into reality.

**DISCUSSION QUESTIONS**

1. If you were the owner of a firm with fifty employees, would you initiate a formal appraisal program? Would you tie pay raises to the results? Would you develop your own instrument?

2. Can you explain why so many supervisors dread formal reviews? Does their attitude keep them from doing a good job of reviewing? Why is it so difficult to judge or evaluate others?

3. Do you agree that employees should complete their own appraisal forms and then let the supervisor react and make changes before submitting the forms to personnel?

# Option

### Objective

To discover the advantages and disadvantages of two different approaches to formal appraisal of employees.

### Problem

Ms. Y and Mr. X are in complete disagreement regarding the best way to appraise their employees. Mr. Big, tired of the conflict, decides to let the five employees in Supervisor Joe's department resolve it.

### Players

All five nonmangagement roles.

### Procedure

Everyone in the class or seminar reads the material below. The five players then discuss the advantages and disadvantages of each approach from their point of view as employees being appraised. After the discussion they vote on the approach (Ms. Y or Mr. X) they prefer. Nonplayers win the game if they vote in advance for the preferred approach.

### Ms. Y's Technique

Ms. Y prefers the nondirective, soft approach. She likes to sit down in a nonthreatening manner and quietly discuss and settle on the rating of each factor without any advance preparation from either party. She feels that when employees fill out their own appraisal in advance, they tend to defend each rating they give themselves, and the interview may turn into an argument. Her approach is to ask the employee what rating she or he feels is right. If she agrees, they move on quickly; if not, they talk it over. Ms. Y frequently gives in, but she argues that her concession is not a "white wash" job. She believes that through open discussion employees sense their own shortcomings. Other pressures are not necessary. Her ratings are consistently higher than those of Mr. X.

### Mr. X's Technique

Mr. X takes a more directive, hard approach. He follows the procedure of giving the appraisal instrument to each employee a few days in advance, asking that it be completed and brought to the interview at the scheduled time. In the meantime he spends considerable time completing the same form independently. The interview consists of comparing forms and adjusting differences. When Mr. X feels he is right, he takes a firm stand and presents all possible data to back up his lower or higher rating. He does, however, make some adjustments when justified. He is always complimentary on high ratings, strives to be fair, and takes time to tie the procedure into long-term career plans.

### Postgame Discussion

Which supervisor would you prefer to rate you? Why? Discuss how each technique might be improved or how a combination of both could be more effective.

# MANAGING YOURSELF

# Establishing Goals

*When you finish this unit, you should be able to (1) write out the planning formula covered in the chapter, (2) describe each part in detail, and (3) adapt it to your own work situation.*

''It's great to be a lowly employee instead of a supervisor because you can report to work without thinking. You know, just stumble in and let the job grab you instead of you grabbing the job. Let the supervisor do the planning, scheduling, and thinking. After all, she's getting paid for it. Let her see to it that you have a productive day.''

The above quotation may not express the best possible employee attitude, but it contains enough truth to cause the supervisor to ask some very pointed questions. If the supervisor doesn't give the department direction, who will? If she or he doesn't organize, plan, schedule, and

**129**

pick up the loose ends, where will such leadership come from? If the supervisor doesn't provide the employee with a good day, who is to blame?

There are some fairly basic differences between the positions of employee and supervisor. The employee can become involved in the activities of the department without worrying over where the department is going. The employee can relax without having to fit what he or she does into a total plan.

The worker can achieve job satisfaction without sweating out reports, plans, figures, purchases, statistics, comparisons, and so forth. The supervisor, on the other hand, must constantly look at the overall picture. Are all employees properly assigned and fully productive? How is the department doing in comparison with others? How much increase in productivity might be expected in the next six months? What cost factors can be eliminated or reduced?

### The Importance of Planning

The role of a supervisor is a far cry from that of an employee. You can't just let things happen but must *make* them happen. You must control a multitude of factors, deal with countless emergencies, and pick up a variety of loose ends, constantly directing and guiding the activities of others. No matter how many details must be faced, no matter how frantic the pace, you must stay on top of the situation.

*Nobody wants to work for an unorganized supervisor.*

How can you do all these things? *By being an organized person with a definite plan.*

Managers must occasionally pull themselves away from the trees so they can see the forest. They must seek isolation and find a quiet time and place where they can plan. The degree to which a manager is successful in doing this will determine the long-range success that he or she might enjoy.

### The Gantt Bar Chart

Henry L. Gantt, an early management consultant, recognized that any sound plan is made up of a number of interlocking projects (smaller plans) that are dependent upon each other and must be molded together under a time limitation. He designed a bar-chart showing the relationship of time to various subprojects in a master plan. Assume you are the owner of a restaurant that needs remodeling, but you do not wish to close down. You might construct Gantt-type chart like the one below to show how the restaurant could be remodeled one section at a time.

### Network Analysis Plan

Production engineers often design highly sophisticated plans when a new product is to be manufactured. A plan that stresses an awareness of each step in a production path is called *network analysis*. A chart clearly identifies each step (some operating simultaneously) in an entire project—one that might take months or years to complete. For example, PERT (Program Evaluation Review Technique) is a well-known system that the U.S. Navy used to save almost two years on a missle project.

Restaurant Remodeling Chart

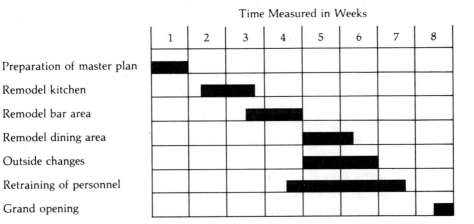

Beginning supervisors do not need such highly complex systems to handle their responsibilities, but they can benefit from a simplified one. The following formula serves this purpose.

$$MO + DP + SP = PS$$

Put into words, it means the following. MO (management objectives) plus DP (departmental plan) plus SP (small plans) equal PS (personal success). Each symbol in this formula will take on a special meaning as you continue toward becoming a more organized supervisor.

**Formula for Successful Planning**

All supervisory planning should start with top management objectives (MO). These are the broad goals of the company that you sometimes find stated in employee handbooks or in annual reports to stockholders. Management objectives, or goals, can be expressed in terms of service standards, sales volume, profit pictures, or similar criteria and will change from time to time. Sometimes the supervisor may have a small voice in forming these broad objectives, but most of the time the supervisor must take responsibility for goals handed down from higher management and must then relate the operation of the department to

**Management by Objectives**

the company goals. In so doing, the supervisor should ask these questions:

1. What are the current objectives of my company?
2. How might my department contribute more in reaching these objectives?
3. Is my department doing anything not in conformity with these goals?

Departmental Plans

Obviously management objectives are never reached unless they are implemented with actual productivity within reach of the smaller divisions making up the organization. So *DP* is added to the formula because a department cannot contribute significantly to management objectives without a plan of its own. This is where you come into the picture.

You should develop your own departmental plan, gear it toward broad management objectives, and then interpret it for your own employees.

Departmental plans can take many forms, so you may receive considerable help from your manager in building your plan. She or he may ask you for a monthly, semiannual, or yearly written plan, provide the necessary forms, and give you a model to work from. On the other hand, if your manager does not ask you for a plan, you may prepare one exclusively for your own purposes. In either case, you should have a plan that includes at least the following features.

1. Make your plan workable, because an impossible goal does not motivate.
2. Make your plan flexible so you can adjust to changes beyond your control.
3. Include all elements or factors over which you have control.
4. State the expected increase in productivity (tangible, sales, or service) in clear terms. Always include previous figures for comparison.
5. Tie your plan to management objectives.

A workable departmental plan is not easy to develop. It will take time, effort, and some heavy thinking on your part, but without it you have no direction. The kind of plan you develop will depend upon many variables that cannot be discussed here.

At any rate, let's assume you now have a departmental plan. It contains the broad objectives you hope to reach in your department in the next six months or year. It states the things you hope to achieve so that your department will show growth and improvement, and will make its maximum contribution to the company as a whole. If you can accomplish these goals, or come close to them, your reputation as a manager will be greatly enhanced. Once you set these goals, you have committed yourself. Management may not hold you firmly to them but managers will probably refer to them from time to time.

We now come to the next part of the formula, the *SP*, or small plans. You cannot, of course, reach the goals of your overall plan unless you make it work by dividing it into little plans that are achievable on a daily or weekly basis. In short, you need a continuous supply of small plans or goals to augment your major departmental plan. Many experienced supervisors develop a daily checklist (tied to departmental plans), which they follow as closely as the situation permits.

**Small Plans**

   "While driving to work in the morning, I organize my day by making up a list of things to do. When I get to my desk, I write this list on my calendar pad and assign priorities. I then spend the rest of the day trying to check them off. It works for me."

   "I never leave work, even if I'm late, until I have a priority list of things to do when I show up the next day. This makes it easier for me to leave my problems at work and gives me a good starting point the next day. I'd recommend it to the beginning supervisor."

   "For the last twenty years I've made it a practice to show up fifteen minutes early every morning so I can organize my daily plan. I find I can sort things out more clearly this time of day."

   Small daily plans eventually add up to the successful completion of overall departmental plans. The daily checklist is an excellent practice and is strongly recommended for both the new and experienced supervisor. The key to such a list is setting up the right priorities and following certain rules. (Setting priorities will be discussed in Chapter 14.) It must be emphasized, however, that the only worthwhile goals are *reachable* goals. That is why small, short, and immediate goals make sense. Some supervisors divide their small plans into daily and weekly classifications. A weekly goal might include something that takes more than one day to accomplish, such as changing a basic procedure, rearranging an office, or contacting a series of customers. A daily goal might include taking someone to lunch, counseling with an employee who seems unhappy, finishing a report, or similar activities.

Personal success is a combination of many factors and personal characteristics, but *being an organized person* is certainly one of them. This is especially true of supervisors, because only those who can organize a small department can organize a larger operation. The sooner you demonstrate to your superiors that you have the ability to organize

**Personal Success**

yourself and your department, the sooner you will start your climb up the organizational ladder.

As a way of review, let's now apply the formula to a single case involving JoAnn, a young bank manager. She has been a manager for only a short time and has been charged with the responsibility of opening up a branch in an enclosed shopping center. How might the formula apply to her?

*Management Objectives (MO).*   JoAnn works for a state-wide banking operation which has four basic goals at this point: (1) to expand until they have 200 branches, (2) to improve profits so they can declare a bigger dividend for stockholders, (3) to improve their image as a friendly financial institution that takes a personal interest in all people, and (4) to improve their cultural mix of employees and to bring more women into top management. JoAnn feels strongly that her small branch (only nine employees) can contribute to these company-wide objectives.

*Departmental Plans (DP).*   A few weeks before she opened her branch JoAnn was required to submit a plan for the first six months of operation. It was based to some extent on what other new branches the same size and in similar situations had experienced. It included the following: (1) the date when she hoped the operation would become profitable, (2) deposit and loan figures she hoped to achieve, stated monthly, and (3) a customer relations plan that she hoped would satisfy all clients, especially those business organizations within the shopping center that would depend heavily upon her bank.

*Small Plans (SP).*   JoAnn has her own system when it comes to small action plans or goals. Each weekend (usually at home) she develops a few weekly goals. She writes them in her appointment notebook but never shares them with anyone. They include goals such as: (1) special public relations efforts such as calling on a few key clients, (2) getting reports to the head office in better shape and before deadlines, (3) planning a short staff meeting, (4) a training job that needs to be done. But JoAnn does not let it go at that—she also uses a daily goal system. Every morning when she arrives and opens the bank (she tries to beat everyone else by twenty minutes), she sits down and writes on her desk calendar the smaller things she wants to accomplish before she goes home. Often there are deadlines or time orders for these priorities. Some of these she has thought about enroute to work so it takes only a few minutes to write them down. She may add one or two during the day, but she makes an effort to check them off as she goes. Here again it is a private matter with her. On days when she completes all her small goals, she has a great inner feeling. Sometimes, of course, she must postpone a few until the next day because things were so hectic that she couldn't get around to them.

Implementation of the formula—as simple as it may be—can convert a disorganized, unsuccessful supervisor into an organized, successful one. If JoAnn desires to move into a higher position at a later date, she is smart to adapt the formula to her own style.

Here are some final tips that will help you put it into operation:

*Keep your departmental plans simple.* A departmental plan is simply a proposed blueprint or map for the future. An ultra-sophisticated plan may look pretty, but it might not be workable. Keep it simple and attainable.

*Organize yourself on a daily basis.* Most supervisors need a simple procedure to follow each day in order to accomplish first things first and follow through on other activities. The daily checklist is a worthwhile tool.

*Achieve results through people.* Your departmental plan and your daily checklist are useless unless you put them into action through people. This means you must develop your human relations skills to make your plan work.

The full significance of the formula and the whole idea of planning may become more meaningful to you after you read the next two chapters, which are designed to help you put your plans into operation.

1. Would you like to be a supervisor in a corporation that subscribes to and firmly practices the Management by Objectives (M.B.O.) philosophy? Defend your position whether you answer yes or no.

2. Do you agree that when supervisors prepare their own written plans (with little or no pressure from management) they are more likely to translate the plan into motivating goals?

3. Do you agree with a popular idea that a college student who takes a full academic load, works about twenty hours a week, and tries to lead a social life, is automatically being trained to become an organized person and is therefore receiving management training whether or not she or he is taking a supervision course?

**DISCUSSION QUESTIONS**

# Planning

Mr. Big is a strong, almost obsessed, proponent of personal planning and organization. He uses an elaborate system of daily, weekly, and long-term goals for himself. He uses a personal computer at home for both personal and business purposes. He believes that organization is the best form of personal discipline, and that goal setting is the most motivating thing a person can do. Each night, before he leaves work, he writes all of his goals for the following day on a desk pad. He spends some time each weekend at home setting goals. A fanatical believer in M.B.O., he always submits a highly complex plan to his superiors, and always on time. He gets satisfaction from checking off a written goal when it has been accomplished.

Ms. Y is also a strong believer in goal setting and good organization, but her approach is flexible and unstructured. She does not follow any specific formula and she never writes anything down. Rather, she keeps a changing and shifting master plan in her mind. She constantly revises it when driving on the freeway, or having a drink at home, or waiting in line at her bank. Ms. Y does not think much of M.B.O. She claims it takes too much time to prepare a plan, that upper management ignores most of the plans submitted, and that changes make them obsolete almost immediately. She also believes that too much structure keeps one from being creative.

Do you support Mr. Big or Ms. Y? Defend your position. Would you recommend a compromise?

# Setting Priorities

*If you study this chapter, you should be able to accomplish one of the following: (1) noticeably improve your priority alignment as a supervisor or (2) noticeably improve your educational and personal priority alignments as a nonsupervisor.*

Priorities are a vital part of any plan. In one respect, they *are* the plan. They indicate what you feel is most important and what can be temporarily ignored. Obviously, people who are good at setting up priorities accomplish their plans or goals more easily and efficiently than those who are not.

In putting any plan into operation, you should always concentrate on doing the most urgent tasks first. Just because a particular task comes into your office first doesn't mean it should be handled ahead of other things; just because you didn't have time to do something yesterday doesn't mean it should have top priority today.

A supervisor's priority list should be made up and constantly revised according to sound principles and sound thinking. Setting priorities is a decision-making process whereby you rank in order the tasks that need to be done by you and the people who work for you—first, second, third, and so on down the line. Following such an order in taking care of tasks and problems will help you reach your goals. It's not as easy as it sounds, however. Setting priorities will be one of your major challenges as a supervisor. Listed below are eight questions to ask yourself when setting priorities.

- If I deal with this problem first, will it automatically solve others later?
- If I deal with this problem first, will it delay the solution of another that will eventually cause severe damage to productivity or my career?
- If I delay action on this problem, will it solve itself?
- What can I delegate on my list so that I can get to more serious problems sooner?
- Will taking care of this small problem first free my mind to take care of my number one problem later?
- What tasks must I complete quickly so that I will not hold up the schedule of other people or other departments?
- Can I group a few things together and save time by solving them all at once?
- Is the time psychologically right to take a problem up with my boss or should I wait for a more appropriate time?

You can see that setting priorities is a complex, demanding process that you can never perfect. Yet the more effective you become at it, the more success you can anticipate. Many managers have learned that keeping a written list of priorities is best for them; others prefer to carry a list around in their minds, a rather fluid list that constantly changes as changes occur in the work environment.

**Advantages of a Written List**

You may have the aptitude that enables you to be skillful at keeping a running priority list in your mind, but most beginning supervisors find it advantageous to write out a list on a desk pad. Here's why.

1. Writing the list is a form of self-discipline. When you know what needs to be done next, you are better organized and less likely to waste time.

2. The list frequently eliminates forgetting, which can get one into trouble with superiors. Some supervisors simply prefer to trust visible lists instead of their memories.

3. Completing a list and checking off items is self-satisfying and motivating. A priority list is, in effect, a personal reward system.

The disadvantages of writing a list are that it takes time, and it causes some supervisors to be overstructured. Once a task is written down, some people experience a reaction of frustration until the job has been accomplished.

The first thing you learn about setting priorities is that the order may not last long. All it takes is a call from your manager, an emergency situation, an unexpected human relations problem, or a mechanical breakdown to force you to make up a new list. A priority list is not a static thing and may need revising many times during a single day. In fact, many supervisors automatically reevaluate their priorities every time they move from one completed task to another. Then, you may ask, why make a list in the first place? The primary reason is to keep all responsibilities, tasks, and problems in view. A priority list should include *all* tasks that need to be done to reach your goals as soon as possible. Obviously, a cardinal mistake would be to leave something off the list that should be on it. But even if your list is complete, you can still make mistakes by putting one task or problem ahead of another. For example, if you spend your time on what should be a lower priority matter, you are neglecting something more crucial, resulting in more harm than benefit. You are therefore making a minus contribution. To illustrate the importance of this concept, look at the following examples:

**Keeping Priority Lists Flexible**

> Sid was a department manager for a major retail chain. Last week it was announced that his store would have its annual inspection by a team of top officials. Sid wanted a good report so badly that he gave top priority to cleaning up and rearranging the department and everything else was neglected. Predictably, Sid and the department received a 100 percent rating. But what happened to the other priorities? For one thing Sid neglected to turn in a merchandise reorder list on time and the department was out of stock on many important items for more than two weeks. Sid—and his company— paid a high price for a poor priority decision. There was, of course, plenty of time for Sid to take care of all his top priorities.

> Gayle was so fed up with the poorly organized files in her department that she finally decided to reorganize them herself, making it her top priority. Once she got into the task, she discovered things were worse and took much longer than she anticipated. As a result, she neglected other important matters including annual reviews of the six people in her department. Personnel was very upset about it. Later, as Gayle thought it over, she realized that if she had taken care of the reviews first, she could have used them to motivate her employees to clean up the files themselves. She permitted her frustration to overemphasize one problem at the expense of another that should have been first priority.

Duke was chief of a repair crew that had been working long hours due to heavy storm conditions. No sooner did they make one repair than they were sent by radio to do another. Each day Duke was supposed to turn in written reports on projects finished, but last Tuesday he wasn't organized, failed to set any priorities, and forgot to turn in the report. As a result, another repair crew was sent a hundred miles away to do a job Duke's crew had already completed. It was an embarrassing situation.

**Effective Priority Setting**

How can you set priorities that will make it easier for you to reach your goals and keep you out of trouble? Here are some suggestions.

*Give priority to any problem that is rendering you ineffective as a supervisor.* Sometimes a very upsetting human relations problem might be bothering you, such as a conflict with one of your employees or a serious communications conflict with your superior. Such situations can disturb you emotionally and make you ineffective or at least not up to standard in the rest of your work.

*Don't focus only on your top priority task.* Frequently supervisors become so involved in reaching one goal that they neglect others, resulting in more harm in the long run. Keep all your priorities in mind and do a balancing act among them to prevent this from happening.

*Sometimes it is good to delay a problem or task, giving it a lower priority.* Some problems become so complicated that an immediate solution is impossible. More time is needed to evaluate the facts and measure the total impact. In such instances, you might wish to drop it to the bottom of your list where you can watch it but not forget it.

*Sometimes you can group goals into a meaningful sequence.* Many supervisors are good at putting their daily goals into a priority pattern that saves time and effort. Into this category fall such things as making one trip accomplish three goals or arranging tasks in sequence so that they are easier to accomplish.

*If something has been on your list for a long time, either do it, or forget it.* An item that keeps showing up on a priority list soon becomes an irritant. Don't let this happen.

*Don't push what should be a high priority item to the bottom of your list because of fear.* Some managers keep what should be top priority items under cover because they are afraid to face them. This is a serious mistake because time solves very few problems.

*Oscillating back and forth from one priority to another is unwise.* Once you put a task near the top of your list, try to complete it within a reasonable space of time. If you start something and then keep switching to another priority, you will lose all motivation to complete the project.

**How to Get Started**

If setting up a priority list is a new experience for you, the following tips will help you get started. Later, after you have had additional experience, you can adopt the process to your own individual style. If you are not currently a supervisor, you may wish to set up a personal priority list.

1. Select the task or project that will, in your opinion, advance the productivity of your department the most, and put it at the top of your list. Leave it there until it is completed or a more important task surfaces.

2. List two additional tasks or projects that are less important but should still be number two and three on your pad. Frequently there is less time pressure on these.

3. List, in succession, any tasks (reports, appointments, telephone calls, counseling) that either must or should be accomplished before you leave work.

4. Select and list a ''fun'' project— something you could look forward to doing as an end-of-the-day personal reward—near the bottom or end of your list.

5. Try to restrict the number of tasks on your list to around seven. Too many priority projects can lead to confusion and demotivation. Even though it may be your goal to accomplish as much as possible in a single day, there is always tomorrow. Those who over-schedule themselves take the risk of turning out poor quality work with higher levels of frustration.

Check off your priority list and prepare a new one at the end of the day. You will transfer some unfinished tasks to the new list, realign them, and add new ones. This process accomplishes two psychological goals: First, it helps you leave your responsibilities at work so you will be free to enjoy your leisure time. Second, arriving at work the following day with a list already prepared saves time and can be self-motivating.

Setting priorities for personal tasks off the job can be as important as those at work. If you use what you have learned in this chapter in both environments, you will automatically do a better job of balancing home and career.

1. Do you agree with the concept that those who do not keep a written priority list needlessly burden their minds?

**DISCUSSION QUESTIONS**

2. Do supervisors who improve their priority decisions automatically improve the quality of their other decisions? In short, is there a carry-over?

3. What is the relationship between setting long-term goals and setting daily priorities? How does priority setting fit into the formula presented in Chapter 13?

*Do not turn this page until told to do so.*

# Priorities

**Problem**

To provide simulated experience in setting priorities under pressure.

**Problem**

You (Supervisor Joe) left Monday morning for a one-week company-sponsored training program in supervisory leadership. Your department was turned over to Mrs. R, but she became ill and went home. You were called to return on an emergency basis and arrived five minutes ago. The time is 1:00 P.M. Friday. As you walk into your work station, you face ten critical problems.

**Procedure**

These problems are listed on the following page. Read, evaluate, and assign a priority number to each problem. In other words, decide which problem you would handle first, second, third, and so forth. You have only three minutes to do this, and you cannot start until you receive a signal from the group leader.

Once you receive the signal, turn the page and read all ten problems. You are then ready to assign the priority numbers in the appropriate squares in the left-hand column. While participants are making their priority choices, the instructor or trainer should list the choices in abbreviated form on a blackboard so that results can be compared. When the time is up, the instructor should invite one individual at a time to put her or his priority list on the board and defend it in front of the group.

**Players**

Everyone plays the role of Supervisor Joe.

PRIORITY LIST

☐  A formal grievance from Mrs. R is on your desk.  To read and digest it would take 15 minutes.

☐  Mr. Big has left word that he wants to see you in his office immediately upon your return.  Anticipated time:  60 minutes.

☐  You have some very important looking unopened mail (both company and personal) on your desk.  Time:  10 minutes.

☐  Your telephone is ringing.

☐  A piece of equipment has broken down, halting all production in your department.  You are the only one who can fix it.  Anticipated time:  30 minutes.

☐  Someone is seated outside your office waiting to see you.  Time:  10 minutes.

☐  You have an urgent written notice in front of you to call a Los Angeles operator.  Both your mother and the company headquarters are located in Los Angeles.  Time:  10 minutes.

☐  Mr. X has sent word he wants to see you and has asked that you return his call as soon as possible.  Time:  10 minutes.

☐  Mrs. Q is in the women's lounge and claims to be sick.  She wants your permission to go home.  It would take about 5 minutes to get the facts and make a decision.

☐  In order to get to your office by 1:00 you had to miss lunch.  You are very hungry, but you figure it will take 30 minutes to get something substantial to eat.

**Postgame Discussion**

Discussion should center on the differences between priority patterns put on the blackboard. Why might one be better than another? Should the broken equipment have received priority on all lists? Did anyone save time by grouping? Are some people intimidated by a telephone or their boss?

# Managing Your Time

*If you complete the exercises in this chapter and integrate the changes indicated into your behavior patterns, you should achieve a noticeable improvement in the management of your time.*

If you establish sound goals for your department and yourself and learn to set priorities on a daily basis, will you automatically become more effective at managing your time? Not necessarily. You still need to deal with the basic problem of time allocation itself.

Why should you make a special effort to manage your time?

*You will spend fewer hours working.* Some managers do not seem to be able to do their jobs during regular working hours and must arrive early in the morning and take work home at night. Usually they blame the

**Advantages of
Time Management
145**

company itself: "They throw too much work at you. Too much paper. Too many problems. You'd have to be a magician to handle it all during regular hours." Those who make such statements forget that problems, tasks, and reports cannot organize themselves. This kind of organization is the primary reason a supervisor is needed in the first place. After a manager has been in a position for a few months, extra hours are justified only under special or emergency conditions. Otherwise, the supervisor should blame his or her own inability to manage time, not the workload involved.

*You will be less frustrated.* A good manager senses and handles problems before they get out of hand. When you learn to manage your time well, you can prevent fires rather than spending more time putting them out. Because you are on top of your job—not always catching up—productivity is more even, there are fewer emergencies and unpleasant surprises, and you have fewer problems to handle. In short, you need to manage time well so that you can create the extra time you need to be a manager.

*You will have the time you need to prepare for the future.* Until you learn to organize and manage your time well enough to take on additional responsibilities, you are not promotable. You cannot prepare for the next position if you are bogged down with your present job. You cannot do a good job of personal career development if you habitually operate on a crisis basis. You must *make* more time now through better time management to prepare for a bigger role in the future.

Despite his young age and modest formal education, Frank is a successful, highly respected executive in a demanding field. He has time to play racketball each day, never neglects his family, devotes time to his church, takes care of personal business matters, and still has time left over for social and personal leisure activities. How does he do it? *Frank manages his time.* If you could meet with him and you asked the right question he might supply the following answers.

**How to Manage Your Time**

*Change your attitude toward time.* "Learn to value your on-the-job time more fully. For a long time I didn't worry how long it took me to do things, but then I suddenly realized I was spending more hours than necessary on certain assignments. As a matter of fact, I was spending more time than was necessary on the job itself because it was beginning to encroach on my leisure time and influence my personal lifestyle. I soon realized that time was one thing I couldn't stretch. I was expected to complete my work in eight hours. If I didn't, it was my fault, not the job's or the company's. The only alternative to better time management was to dip into my personal time. It was then that I decided that time *could* be managed. Know what I discovered? If you learn to manage your working hours, you seem to enjoy your nonworking hours more.''

*Delegate more.* ''The best way to save your own time is to let somebody else do the task. Many managers could save far more time than they think if they delegated more effectively. Nothing is more revealing than to see a manager who is overworked while his people are underworked. Yet it happens frequently.''

*Look for and take shortcuts.* ''There is usually more than one way to complete a task. Try to find the best way and the one that takes the least amount of time. Could you get people to come to see you instead of taking the extra time to go to see them? Would a written note to a superior in advance of a meeting help you accomplish more in less time when you arrive? Could you set up a luncheon meeting to accomplish a business goal and still enjoy it? Could you save time by discussing the problem with an expert instead of struggling with it too long yourself? You will manage your time better if you use a little more of it to figure out the fastest route to get where you are going.''

*Group tasks together.* ''If you watch a supervisor who has learned to manage time well, you will discover that little jobs and tasks are grouped together so they can be accomplished at the same time. A trip or meeting might be delayed until it can accomplish more than one thing; a trip to the executive offices in the same building can be planned so that the mail can be picked up, a report dropped off, and an executive seen all in one trip instead of three; five or six people can be brought together to save time on communication; a list can be made in advance so that a counseling session will cover everything and make a follow-up unnecessary. Sometimes a manager has developed the skill to do more than one thing at the same time without offending others. When stalled on the telephone, the supervisor might read some official publications; a business matter might be introduced while walking to another meeting; when a dull staff meeting is tied up on a problem that does not involve the supervisor, he or she might plan a priority list for the next day.''

*Eliminate the little time-wasters.* ''Some manufacturing plants do micro-time and motion studies on their production employees. Employees are filmed doing their work, and then they carefully view their motions in an attempt to eliminate unnecessary activities. Perhaps this would be a good technique with supervisors. A film would probably show you many ways to save time through elimination of needless motions or activities.''

If you wish to benefit from Frank's suggestions, take a close look at your present habits through the time-waster assessment scale that follows. As you complete it, keep in mind that in controlling your time more effectively, you do not want to squeeze all the joy out of your job. Your goal is to use your time wisely so that you will enjoy your job more, not less.

---

## SUPERVISOR'S TIME-WASTER ASSESSMENT SCALE

Circle the number that best indicates where you lie between the two extremes. Total your score at the end of the exercise.

| | | | | | | |
|---|---|---|---|---|---|---|
| When I arrive at work in the morning, I get started immediately. | 5 | 4 | 3 | 2 | 1 | It takes me at least 30 minutes to get started in the morning. |
| I do not procrastinate; my priority list prevents delay. | 5 | 4 | 3 | 2 | 1 | I procrastinate because I never know what to do next. |
| I keep personal activities to an absolute minimum. | 5 | 4 | 3 | 2 | 1 | I let personal activities eat away my on-the-job time. |
| My schedule is rigid; I never overextend a coffee or lunch break. | 5 | 4 | 3 | 2 | 1 | Three-hour nonbusiness lunches and 40-minute coffee breaks are common with me. |
| I'm an extremely fast reader and I waste no time on trash mail. | 5 | 4 | 3 | 2 | 1 | I need a reading-improvement course; I waste too much time reading. |
| My telephone conversations are to the point and deal only with business matters. | 5 | 4 | 3 | 2 | 1 | I socialize on the telephone—my number one time-waster. |
| I delegate as many tasks as possible. | 5 | 4 | 3 | 2 | 1 | Failure to delegate is a serious problem with me. |
| I refuse to let others waste my time in pointless conversations. | 5 | 4 | 3 | 2 | 1 | When people use up my time just chatting, I can't seem to break away. |
| I don't waste a single minute oversupervising. | 5 | 4 | 3 | 2 | 1 | Oversupervising is killing my time-management plan. |
| I schedule my appointments so that I waste no time waiting. | 5 | 4 | 3 | 2 | 1 | I often keep either myself or others waiting. |
| I stay motivated until I go home. | 5 | 4 | 3 | 2 | 1 | "Afternoon drag" slows me down to a crawl. |
| My objectives are clear; I know where I am going. | 5 | 4 | 3 | 2 | 1 | My objectives are fuzzy; I often go in the wrong direction. |
| I socialize on the job only after the day's objectives have been reached. | 5 | 4 | 3 | 2 | 1 | I look for opportunities to socialize to escape from work. |
| I have no pet projects; I stick to my priority list. | 5 | 4 | 3 | 2 | 1 | I can't stay away from some time-wasting pet projects. |
| I counsel my employees but never become overinvolved. | 5 | 4 | 3 | 2 | 1 | Every time I counsel an employee I become overinvolved. |
| I avoid mistakes by working steadily at an even tempo. | 5 | 4 | 3 | 2 | 1 | I make foolish mistakes by hurrying to catch up. |

SUPERVISOR'S SCALE (continued)

| | | | | | | |
|---|---|---|---|---|---|---|
| My priority list and general attitude eliminate crisis management. | 5 | 4 | 3 | 2 | 1 | I'm always putting out fires and operating in a crisis. |
| I maintain a highly efficient personal filing system. | 5 | 4 | 3 | 2 | 1 | My personal filing system is a time-wasting mess. |
| I ask for help with tough problems that consume time. | 5 | 4 | 3 | 2 | 1 | I would rather solve my own problem no matter how long it takes. |
| I make maximum use of time-saving equipment such as computers and copying machines. | 5 | 4 | 3 | 2 | 1 | Doing things the old-fashioned way gives me more personal satisfaction. |

TOTAL POINTS ☐

If you scored yourself over 90 you are a highly organized supervisor and you waste almost no time. If you scored yourself between 70 and 90, you need some slight improvement. If, however, you scored yourself under 70, you would probably enjoy your work more and improve your future by eliminating some needless, perhaps frustrating, time-wasters.

---

Now that you have completed the Time-Waster Assessment Scale you may wish to log your time among various activities for a typical day. This approach (using the EIGHT-HOUR-DAY INVENTORY ANALYSIS CHART on the next page) will help you compare the actual time you spend with the time you *should* spend.

Here are Frank's final comments: "Look, work is work. There is no way to make pure fun out of it. Certainly I want to enjoy my work as much as anyone, but I don't want it to drag on. I like to dispose of my work responsibilities with pride, vigor, and efficiency. My approach is to be professional, so when I get to work, I assume a 'let's get it done' attitude. I use my time in an orderly manner and my employees pick up the tempo. Then sometimes we take a real break and relax. I learned a long time ago that the only way to enjoy a little fun time on the job is to control your time so well that there is some to spare. Then it feels good. There is no other answer. You have time working for you, not against you."

**DISCUSSION QUESTIONS**

1. Do you agree or disagree with the concept that you have to invest a little time to save a lot of time? Explain.

2. What signals might a supervisor receive when his or her time is managed poorly? What signals might be received when activities are overorganized?

3. Do you support the idea of taking a daily time inventory to improve time management? Is logging time for only one day sufficient? Should time be logged during or at the end of the day?

---

**EIGHT-HOUR-DAY
INVENTORY ANALYSIS CHART**

| Activity | Time Spent in Minutes | Optimum Time in Minutes (your opinion) |
|---|---|---|
| Paperwork (reports, correspondence) | | |
| Inspection or actual supervision | | |
| Communication (counseling) | | |
| Actually working yourself | | |
| Command meetings (imposed by management) | | |
| Problem solving | | |
| Planning | | |
| Other _____ | | |
| Other _____ | | |
| Other _____ | | |
| TOTAL | | |

1. Add both columns.
2. Subtract "time spent" from "optimum time." The difference is time wasted.

# Analysis

Supervisor Joe has been working extra hours to catch up on everything he needs to do in his department. No matter how he tries to save time, he never catches up. As a result, Joe has become increasingly irritable, haggard, and ineffective. Unable to solve the problem, Joe makes an appointment with Mr. Big, then makes a big pitch for an assistant to help release the pressure. But Mr. Big replies that better time management would solve Joe's problem. He asks Joe to write down how he spent his time yesterday.

Read Joe's inventory on the next page. How is he wasting time? What specific changes would you suggest to him?

## JOE'S TIME INVENTORY

| Activity | Time | Activity | Time |
|---|---|---|---|
| Preparing written request to Mr. Big attempting to justify a 20 percent increase in budget next year. | 60 min. | Typed up five extra copies of a productivity report so that all five employees would be informed. | 30 min. |
| Discussing next month's production schedule with Mr. G; will do same with Mrs. R, Mr. K, and Miss Q later. | 15 min. | Struggled again with a new layout plan that would free about forty square feet for a new piece of equipment on order. Got disgusted and tore up new and previous plans. Impossible. | 50 min. |
| Handling thirteen telephone calls only three of which were personal. | 50 min. | Trip to union hall to talk to our agent about a grievance that had been continuing too long. Meeting took thirty minutes. Transportation time twenty minutes each way. | 70 min. |
| Worked in stockroom alone doing a reorganizing job. Left note so that Ricardo would understand. | 50 min. | | |
| Interviewing woman sent by Personnel as a possible replacement for Miss Q, who is leaving in two weeks. Decided individual not suitable. | 50 min. | Waited twenty minutes to see Mr. Big to discuss time-management problem. Conversation lasted ten minutes. | 30 min. |
| Repairing broken equipment that only I could fix. I asked Mr. K and Mr. G to take an early lunch while I repaired it so they could continue working when they returned. | 60 min. | | |

# Make Decisive Decisions

*If you read and apply the ideas in this chapter, you should improve your decision-making abilities to a noticeable degree.*

How would you react to the following advertisement if you found it in your favorite newspaper?

---

**FOR SALE**

**Supervisor's Problem-Solving Machine**

Guarantees Better Decisions with Less Worry

Easy to Use!                                        No Tricks!

Write Scientific Systems for Further Details

---

You would probably be highly skeptical and quickly pass it off as an unethical come-on or a joke. And you would be right. There is no such thing as a surefire decision-making device for supervisors. The great majority of decisions that you are paid to make as supervisor must be made in your mind and not by gadgets, gimmicks, or even sophisticated computers. There are, however, some things you can do to improve your decisions.

You can learn how to make decisions more systematically and train yourself to think through problems more logically. You can remember to take into consideration all factors that should influence the decision. In other words, you can become methodical. Making decisions (problem solving) is no job for a scatterbrained amateur, an impulsive individual who overreacts to every problem, or a person who sees only the surface of the problem. It takes emotional stability, a logical mind, and deep thinking to come up with sound answers to tough problems. This point is illustrated by some sample management comments.

> "I'd make Helen a supervisor tomorrow if she could only learn to make clear-cut decisions instead of being so wishy-washy about every little problem."

> "We finally had to transfer Drew back to his old job. He had great potential as a supervisor, but when it came to making even simple decisions, he fell apart. Fear and frustration took over and everyone lost confidence in him."

> "Gregg keeps getting into hot water because he makes impulsive decisions instead of using his head. His career is grounded until he puts more thought into his decision making."

As a supervisor, you'll find that each day a constant variety of large and small problems will come to you from all directions. You can use one of the following three approaches in dealing with them.

1. You can stall or delay action through any number of often-used ploys. For example, you can bury the problem in red tape, shuffle it in a circle until it disappears, overconsult with your boss until he tells you to forget it, or simply procrastinate until (you hope) a decision is no longer necessary. Using this wishy-washy approach will doom you to failure. Not only will you lose the respect of your superiors, but you will kill the productivity of your employees. The very nature of your job forces you to become a decision maker and there is no escape from the responsibility. You will be expected to make good decisions, but good or bad, they must be made. Except in unusual cases, stalling or delaying will only compound the original problem.

2. You can temporarily dispose of your problems by spilling quick decisions off the top of your head with little or no thinking and even less logic. If you adopt this approach, you will do the following:
   a. use your hunches instead of your rational powers
   b. refuse to consider side effects
   c. give each problem (large or small) the same off-the-cuff treatment.

   If you take this road, you will create more problems than you solve. You will survive for a while, but in the end you'll drown in your own confusion.

3. You can be professional in your approach and learn to solve your many problems through sound decision-making practices. This means following a system, using logical steps, and thinking. It is not easy, but it is the only way you can make decisions that will contribute to greater departmental productivity, that will be enthusiastically accepted by the people who work for you, and that will build a good reputation for you with management.

Supervisors make three kinds of decisions. The *autocratic decision* is one that you make by yourself. You do not consult anyone, and you accept full responsibility for the consequences of your decision. Your second choice is talking over the problem with another person, perhaps a more experienced superior. The result is called a *consultive decision*. Two heads are frequently better than one when a serious decision must be made. It is foolish to make a poor decision on your own if a consultant is available to help you make a better one. The *group decision* is a third possibility. When a problem involves the entire staff, they should participate in the decision, especially if their own decision will satisfy them better and motivate them more.

Regardless of the pattern you use, a logical approach to the decision-making processes itself is essential. You may find the six-step procedure on the next page will fit into your personal comfort zone. If so, embrace it and use it whenever appropriate. Its use can measurably improve your decision-making track record.

Often it is best to take a few seconds to decide what is involved in a decision before you start applying any logical procedure. Like taking a trip, you need to stop and figure out how to proceed. (Consider this step the "decision before making the decision.") For example, to many supervisors it is helpful to divide problems into those that are job-oriented and those that are people-oriented. Once they make this preliminary decision, they can apply the six-step procedure.

---

### SIX-STEP DECISION-MAKING MODEL

Assume that you have accepted a new position with an organization located some miles away in an unfamiliar urban area. While studying a map at your kitchen table, you decide to experiment with the six-step method. Here's what might happen.

| STEPS | EXAMPLE |
|---|---|
| 1. Define desired outcome. | There are at least three different routes you might take. You want the best one. |
| 2. Establish decision criteria. | You want the shortest, fastest, safest route; the one that will cause the least wear and tear on your car and use the least gas. |
| 3. Define alternatives. | Mark off what appear to be the three best routes on your map. |
| 4. Get all the facts. | You will measure the time, number of stops, gas usage, traffic density, and other factors on each route. You will drive a different route each day for three successive days. |
| 5. Weigh and compare. | Compare all facts and opinions to decide which route is best under all conditions. |
| 6. Opt for the best alternative. | Once you have *thought it through*, you can make the decision with confidence. |

---

**Job-Oriented Problems**

There are basically two kinds of job-oriented problems: small problems that require quick answers but have little permanent influence on department operations and major problems that have deep and lasting influence. Most of your decision making will deal with small job problems that you should be able to handle on the spot. Where should this new item be stored? Which report should be completed first? Should I delegate this task or do it myself? Which color would be best? Should I write or telephone my answer?

**Low-Consequence Work-Oriented Decisions**

Most job-oriented decisions the front-line supervisor makes are low on the consequence scale. Even a bad decision will have little impact on productivity or the image of the supervisor. Faulty low-consequence decisions are usually easy to correct. Generally speaking, small problems can be solved immediately and then forgotten. They should be disposed of in an orderly and efficient manner without consuming too much time. The major threat with these problems is that they may become psychological hangups for the supervisor. This can happen when a clear-cut decision is not obvious and, through indecision, the supervisor permits the problem to become a major source of frustration. This kind of distortion is a luxury the supervisor cannot afford. The following half-minute procedure will help you make quick, frustration-free, low-consequence decisions.

1. Take time to restate the problem and review the facts in your mind (should take about ten seconds).

2. Compare the first answer you think of with one or two other possibilities. Weigh one against the other and try to come up with the best choice. If a decision is not obvious, make one anyway (about fifteen seconds).

3. With confidence that you have made the right decision, announce it to those involved and move on to something else (about five seconds).

It is a serious mistake to make a big thing out of a low-consequence decision. You will lose the respect of your superiors and the confidence of your employees. Recognize a small problem for what it is, give it the recommended treatment above, trust your judgment, and then move on to something more important.

Major job-oriented problems that will have a permanent influence on the operation of your department, on the other hand, must be given more serious treatment and more time. These problems probably challenge existing policies or procedures or involve changes in technology, lay-out, design, reporting methods, procedural patterns, control systems, safety rules, or basic production methods. They are major because they touch on something basic in the department and because there are probably complicating side effects. Job-connected problems of this nature and scope deserve careful attention and your best logical thinking. When they occur, lean heavily on the six-step procedure and these additional suggestions.

**High-Consequence Work-Oriented Decisions**

1. *Avoid the temptation to make a quick decision.* Gather all the available facts even if it means making a major project out of it. Ask yourself these questions: What has been done in the past? Why isn't it working today? Will a new system or approach work better? What is the real source of the problem? What are the other factors? Write down all these facts so that you clearly see the detailed overall picture.

2. *If you decide to make an autocratic decision, write down and study each possible solution.* Slowly eliminate those that do not conform to

company policy or have side effects that might do more damage than good. Reduce the list to the two or three possibilities that offer the best permanent solution.

3. *If a clear choice is not evident, use the consultive-decision approach.* Ask your superior or a key employee to talk over the remaining solutions. Sometimes possibilities need to be talked over so that the person making the decision can compare one solution with another.

4. *After some careful weighing, choose the solution you feel is best and take it to your immediate superior for his or her reaction and approval.* Tell why you made the decision and what results you expect. If approved, take the time to communicate the decision to all the people involved.

5. *Follow up* to make sure the decision is properly implemented and that misunderstandings are eliminated.

Major job-connected problems should not be solved in haste or under pressure. When they occur, slow down and follow the logical steps outlined above.

**Low-Consequence People Problems**

The most important thing you can learn about decision making is that people problems are quite different from job problems and demand special treatment. Job-connected problems deal with tangibles or procedures that influence people; people-connected problems deal with the people themselves—their disappointments, frustrations, hostilities, and personality conflicts. People problems may stem from job problems but they exist primarily inside the employee, not outside. Approaching people problems requires your most sensitive handling. Success with these problems depends both on a fair decision and on the way you work with the people involved.

People problems fall into two categories: simple employee requests that require only limited decision making, and deep-seated, complicated problems that require considerable time and all the skill you can muster.

Supervisors often receive special requests from employees concerning work schedules, procedures, breaks, and personal matters that are important to the individual but relatively insignificant in the total operation of the department. In most cases, you can listen carefully and give on-the-spot, yes-or-no answer within a few seconds without spending a great deal of time and effort. To play it safe, however, ask yourself these three questions before answering such requests:

1. Is there a written policy that governs such requests? If so, it should apply (except in very unusual cases) and should be carefully explained to the employee.

2. Will granting the request damage relationships with other employees in your department? If so (except in unusual cases), it should be refused and the reasons made clear to the person making the request.

3. Will granting the request seriously endanger the health and safety of others? If so, it should be refused and the reasons given.

When a special request does not violate any company policy, will not damage the supervisor's relationship with others, and will not endanger the safety of others, it should be granted graciously and quickly.

Any people problems other than simple requests should be considered potentially high-consequence problems. They fall into two classifications: (1) those pertaining to one individual only—these problems are usually highly personal and psychological and should concern the supervisor only because they influence productivity; (2) those that involve two or more employees—these often involve friction in the relation between two or more departmental employees and usually affect productivity. Supplement your six-step procedure with the following suggestions:

**High-Consequence People Problems**

1. *Listen carefully to all problems or complaints.*   If something is important to one of your employees, it is also important to you. Do not ignore or belittle any problem no matter how trivial it may seem at the beginning.

2. *People problems usually involve two or more people so always make an effort to gather information from all sides.*   Do not take sides while you are gathering the facts.

3. *Weigh all the facts carefully in your mind before you make a decision.*   Ask yourself these questions: Will the decision be fair to all concerned? Will it violate any company personnel policies? Are there some serious side effects that need consideration? Will the decision violate any human relations principles? Write down two or three possible decisions for careful evaluation before you choose one.

4. *Using good counseling techniques, openly communicate to all parties involved your decision and why you made it.*   Take time. Encourage a two-way conversation. Listen to any negative reactions, but stand firm on your decision.

5. *Follow up by working to restore or rebuild any relationships that may have been temporarily injured because of your decision.*

The group-decision approach can still accomplish a great deal if the supervisor uses it skillfully. When should it be used? (1) When the decision will have an influence on employees; (2) when there is no urgency

**The Group Decision**

in making a decision; (3) when departmental priorities permit, and (4) when you are willing to abide with the decision they make.

Participative management (Theory Y) frequently involves some time-consuming techniques. For example, it often requires discussion to obtain input from employees before a decision can be made; once such input is received, it must be given priority consideration, thus postponing or changing other tasks and using up even more time. Participative management often forces the supervisor to slow down his or her leadership tempo, which many people find almost impossible to do. It is often much more difficult than you might think to put Theory Y into practice. The pressure from upper management to get the work out according to a schedule can make group decisions impractical. Here is how one successful supervisor puts it:

> "When I left college three years ago, I thought I would be a Theory Y person at least 90 percent of the time. I really believed in it because I was convinced that it would improve morale and achieve greater individual productivity. My goal has not been achieved. In fact, I feel good if I am 60 percent Y and 40 percent X. Why? Too often I have deadlines to meet.
>
> "When I can't spare the time, I make autocratic decisions or consult with a single person. Perhaps when I get into middle management, I will be more successful in meeting this goal."

Leadership and decision-making are inseparable. As you start out, do not expect to bat a thousand, but be satisfied with the best average you can achieve, learning as you go. If you make a mistake, do not hesitate to make a second decision to correct it. Nothing will impinge more forcefully upon your upward mobility than your willingness to improve your decision-making style.

Once the decision is ready to be announced, do it in a *decisive* manner. The more confidence you communicate that you have made the *right* decision, the more acceptance it will receive — and the more leadership you will have demonstrated.

**DISCUSSION QUESTIONS**

1. Why do some beginning supervisors find it so difficult to make even minor low-consequence decisions?

2. Challenge or defend the practice of dividing decisions into two categories: job-oriented or people-oriented.

3. Do most supervisors involve their employees in the decision-making process as much as they should? If not, why don't they?

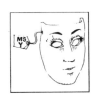

# Termination

## Objective

To provide a simulated experience in evaluating the causes for and potential dangers in termination.

## Problem

Supervisor Joe has made up his mind that he wants to give Mrs. Q the required two-week termination notice. He bases his case on the following: (1) Her productivity dropped about six weeks ago and has never come back up to previous levels. (2) She has been absent twice during this six-week period and late several times. (3) She has, despite suggestions from Supervisor Joe, consistently overextended her coffee breaks. (4) Mrs. R has threatened to quit if Mrs. Q is not transferred out of the department. (5) At 3:30 yesterday afternoon Mrs. Q. walked off the job crying. Mr. Big claims that Supervisor Joe does not have sufficient cause for termination. (1) He has not formally "written up" Mrs. Q twice previously about violations, as required by company policy. (2) Supervisor Joe has not had a heart-to-heart talk with Mrs. Q for two weeks. (3) Although walking off the job is technically cause for dismissal, Mr. Big feels the case has not been fully investigated. (4) He fears that Mrs. Q might appeal her case to the Civil Rights Commission. (5) If the case is not pinned down, Mrs. Q could draw unemployment insurance by contesting the termination procedure (this would cost the company money because it would deplete the reserve fund at the state headquarters).

## Players

All four management roles.

## Procedure

Mr. Big and Supervisor Joe argue the case before Mr. X and Ms. Y, who comprise a two-person jury. After each has presented his case, Mr. X and Ms. Y retire from the room to make their decision. While they are out, those left in the class discuss the situation and vote independently for Mr. Big or Supervisor Joe. You win the game if you agree with the jury.

**Postgame Discussion**

Discussion should center on causes for termination and why business organizations must protect themselves against unfair practices in this area.

# WHERE DO I GO
# FROM HERE?

# Common Mistakes You Don't Want to Make

*When you have completed this chapter, you should be able to improve your up-ward mobility through the elimination of some common mistakes.*

"I've been a personnel director for twelve years and, in my opinion, the greatest mistake most supervisors make is to back away from and be too soft with the employees in their departments. Sometimes you'd think the supervisor is working for the employee and not the other way around."

"I can't help but think that for many supervisors their biggest mistake is old-fashioned stubbornness. They appear to listen to their employees and superiors, but they go right ahead and do it their own way. They lock themselves in with their closed minds."

**165**

"I've been supervising supervisors for more than twenty years with the same company and, in my opinion, their biggest mistake is underestimating the true potential of the people they supervise. They write off people before giving them a chance. This one failure has cost my company millions."

"Most managers multiply their problems because they *think* they communicate with their people when, in fact, they do not. It's their biggest mistake."

If you were to do a survey by asking fifty different management people to name the biggest mistake made by first-line supervisors, you could easily receive twenty or so different answers. But if you examined the essentials of all those responses, they would probably all fit into one of the following categories.

**Failure to Communicate**    Whether they will admit it or not, many supervisors fail to establish and maintain a good communications system within their departments and their company. If the people around you are to become sufficiently informed, you must set up a system to see that it happens. You will have to weave it into your departmental plan and put it on your priority list. You must *make* time to communicate. If you don't you'll be faced with a constant flow of human relations problems from your employees because they will feel left out, neglected, unappreciated, and frustrated. Serious misinterpretations will occur between you and others both inside and outside your department. Morale will eventually drop and so will productivity.

How can you set up a communications system to prevent this from happening? Here are some suggestions.

*Create daily two-way conversations.*    Consider taking ten, twenty, or thirty minutes each day to talk things over with your employees. If you supervise many people, you might rotate among them so that you will have some personal communication at least every week or so. Keep in mind that it is sometimes more important to listen than to talk.

*Set up a bulletin board as a communications headquarters.*    When the proper physical facilities are available, a bulletin board can be a valuable tool. Let's look at how it is used by one supervisor. Linda has trained her nine employees to check the bulletin board the first thing in the morning and two or three times during the day. Sometimes she leaves messages for the whole group, and sometimes for individuals. Employees are, of course, encouraged to leave messages for others, including Linda. Here is how she puts it: "My little bulletin board is an integral part of my system. I just don't have time to contact everyone personally all the time so I write a lot of bulletins and notes. It really works."

*Hold group meetings.*    Try to hold short group meetings from time to time for communication purposes. There is no substitute for the interplay of group communications if such meetings do not take too long, are not over-structured, and are held when necessary. Group meetings are extremely useful when major changes in procedure are necessary.

*Send interoffice communications.*   Most organizations have their own internal mail systems to make it easy for the supervisor to keep upper management, other supervisors, and other staff people informed. This written form of communication should be used to: (1) keep others informed, (2) initiate requests, and (3) reply to inquiries, whether written or by telephone.

*Other communication techniques.*   In addition to the frequent use of the telephone, the supervisor can arrange formal two-way meetings in the office, arrange for luncheon communication sessions, and sometimes take advantage of coffee breaks and trips outside the plant or office for communication purposes.

You will, of course, have to develop your own system based upon your particular situation and needs. The most important factor, however, is to maintain the system on a daily basis. It is a difficult responsibility and no one has created a perfect system, but everyone seems to agree that unless you keep people informed, they can and will misinterpret you, resulting in problems for everyone involved.

## Failure to Exercise Strong Leadership

A shocking number of both new and old supervisors seem reluctant to exercise the kind of forceful leadership management wants, employees respect, and the job requires. Too many supervisors back away from an aggressive employee or avoid any confrontation with those who work for them.

Why? There seem to be several reasons for such behavior. Some supervisors would rather be popular than effective. In other words, they are simply too sensitive to the possibility of receiving a negative reaction from an employee if a firm stand is taken. In other cases, the manager is intimidated by those he or she is supposed to lead. Both responses may stem from a psychological fear of people that needs to be dissipated. Leo is a good example.

Most of the employees in Leo's department loved him. Some said he was the finest supervisor they had ever know. He was kind, sensitive, and calm in all situations. There was a very harmonious climate inside the department most of the time. It naturally came as a shock to the employees when Leo was given a nonsupervisory job and replaced by another man. Why did management take this step? They removed Leo because he was permitting a few employees to take advantage of him. Rules were being broken and production was down. Leo had been counseled on the problem, but couldn't face taking the necessary disciplinary action to correct the situation. As a result, management had no choice but to transfer Leo to a nonsupervisory job.

Some supervisors mistakenly believe that time solves all problems. The people who perpetuate this myth fail to see that one unsolved problem often sets up a chain reaction that creates others. They also fail to recognize that a problem left unsolved can fester and damage a relationship beyond repair. Marge was naive in this respect.

Marge grew up in a home where problems were never dealt with openly. Communication was restricted to pleasant subjects. As a result she formed the habit of keeping most of her personal problems inside. The habit had become so much a part of here that when she became a supervisor she followed the same pattern. What happened? She soon had so many unsolved problems that her boss had to come to her rescue. Solving problems too quickly (without getting the facts) can be a serious mistake, but expecting time to solve them for you is simply going to the opposite extreme.

There are, of course, other reasons why many supervisors fail to provide the strong leadership needed. Some people are much too introverted to communicate their feelings to others. Others have more faith in the behavior of their employees than is justified: a few simply refuse to recognize that the supervisor *must* be a leader to survive. The precautionary measures suggested below will help you avoid such traps.

*Talk about it when it first hits you.* Learn to say what is on your mind when you first have a reaction. There are at least two good reasons to do so; (1) If you don't spill out something that is troubling you as soon as it begins to affect you, it will bother you until it emerges too harshly. The pressure caused by holding it back may put hostility into your voice, leading to misinterpretation. (2) When your employees are permitted some small infraction for a few times, they begin to build a defense against the time when you reprimand them for it. The defense makes them less communicative and sometimes adds an explosive element that would not have been there if you had corrected the infraction at the beginning.

*Say what is on your mind and say it often.* Don't bury your thoughts until they become distorted. Open and frequent communication is an effective way to demonstrate strong leadership.

*Tell it the way it is.* It is a mistake to cushion your verbal communication in soft words and tones so that what you say is taken too lightly or disregarded. Be firm, be clear, and let people know you mean it. Employees can take more frank talk and constructive criticism than you think.

*Let your employees feel that you are leading them.* Most employees like the security of strong leadership from their supervisor. Be considerate, sensitive, and fair—but above all be decisive. If you are, you will dissipate a great deal of apprehenson and confusion among your employees.

*Seek respect rather than popularity.* You will be ill-advised to run a popularity contest in competition with other supervisors. Be content to build honest working relationships based upon the integrity of doing a good job and not upon personal favors that bring immediate gratification but destroy respect. Recognize the difference and you'll be a more successful leader.

A promise can be exciting and ego-building to make but sometimes a distressing impossibility to keep. A promise kept may bring a great deal of inner satisfaction, but a promise broken can be embarrassing and humiliating beyond expectation. Unnecessary promises are too easy to make. The supervisor with a great desire to build good relationships and to increase productivity is prone to make unnecessary promises. For example, John, a very successful supervisor, was so impressed with one of his new employees during the first-month review that he promised the new employee all his support when the time came to appoint a new assistant. Two weeks later (much sooner than John expected) he was forced to appoint someone else as his assistant because the new employee had not served the ninety-day probation period necessary for eligibility. Having to go back on his promise put John in an awkward position. He paid a high price for breaking a promise he didn't need to make in the first place.

**Making and Breaking Promises**

A promise is emotionally accepted. Promises made in a climate of excitement may appear different to you in the cold light of reality, but the changed perspective may not have reached your employees. They fail to understand that busy supervisors with many responsibilities can easily forget a promise even though it was sincerely made. In other words, the receiver sees and feels a promise differently from the giver. The supervisor who ignores this difference is asking for trouble.

Promises easy to keep are also easily forgotten. It is easy to convert a request into a promise and then promptly forget it. For example, an employee might ask you for a special favor such as requisitioning a new inexpensive tool. If you don't do it immediately or write it down to remind yourself to do it later, you may forget it. The world won't end because of your neglect, but sooner or later your poor memory will cause you embarrassment and make it necessary to rebuild a relationship. Even small promises must be kept, and only the organized person who can follow through should make them.

How can you guard against making foolish promises you may not be able to keep? Tell the employee making the request that you can't promise but you'll do everything in your power to make it come about. This helps you avoid making a promise, but it still enables you to support the employee. Don't permit yourself to be carried away by your own enthusiasm so that you make promises that are not expected or needed. You do not have to make promises to create or maintain good relationships with employees.

Of course, you are not expected to avoid completely making promises. Sometimes you must and should make them. Try the following suggestions to help you keep them.

*Write them down.* You'll stand a much better chance of keeping promises if you write them in your notebook or on your desk calendar.

*Admit you might forget.* Tell the employee you intend to keep the promise but you would appreciate a reminder at the appropriate time. This puts some of the responsibility on the employee and helps insure that you'll keep the promise.

*If possible, keep it now.* If you can fulfill a promise before the day is over, do it. It is a mistake to postpone a promise that can be kept immediately.

If, in your role as a supervisor, you can learn to make very few promises but keep those important ones you do make, you will avoid a common and costly mistake.

**Straitjacketing Employees**

Call it prejudging, underestimating, downgrading, or prejudice. Whatever the name, many supervisors put their employees in a psychological straitjacket, preventing them from growing or expanding into the kind of workers they could become. This usually happens because you are unaware of the restrictive climate or barriers you build. You may think you are communicating with the employees but you aren't. There are at least three kinds of supervisors who restrict their employees in this way

*The typecaster.* This is the supervisor who wants to classify and pigeonhole all employees. Rather than accepting and treating everyone as a separate, unique individual, this manager insists upon putting people into groups. For example, he may think that all women who work are first and foremost housewives so he overlooks the professional career woman; he may think all young people prefer not to have early responsibility so he ignores those who do; he may think that all employees work primarily for money so he pays little attention to psychological needs that are often more important than money. There is no way to convince him that by typing people he automatically sets the stage for getting exactly what he expects, no matter how things could have been.

*The snuff-out artist.* This is the supervisor who squelches the ambition and creativity of employees without knowing it by having an overpowering demeanor which may include a gruff voice, using a bulldozer approach, or adhering to a stiff, militaristic style. This supervisor's personality is so powerful that he or she snuffs out the sparks of creativity in employees.

*The poor perceiver.* This is the supervisor who is not sensitive enough to see the potential that lies dormant within employees. He or she doesn't see hidden talent and therefore fails to recognize a special contribution that deserves a compliment, and doesn't recognize improvement in a new employee and thereby fails to reinforce it. The poor perceiver does not recognize and treat employees as separate individuals because he or she does not see their differences. When this happens, employees recognize it and give up.

How can you guard against putting your employees in straitjackets? How can you train yourself to bring out the potential of your employees instead of restricting it? Here are three suggestions that may help.

*Take time to know your employees.* Occasionally relax for a few moments with each employee during coffee breaks or other informal sessions so that you can better perceive and understand their special needs and individual persnalities. What are their interests and ambitions? Are they going to school part time? Gaining insight into individuals as people instead of as employees will help you avoid putting anyone in a psychological straitjacket.

*Look for potential first and performance second.* Although all employees must be judged on their performance, it is a mistake to evaluate performance without first looking at the individual's potential. Most employees have an undiscovered skill, talent, or aptitude that could be used in their work if they were encouraged to use it. Discover and encourage the use of hidden abilities of those who work for you.

*Give employees the confidence they need to take advantage of the opportunities you provide.* To realize their potentials, most employees need large doses of confidence that only you can provide. Sometimes this will mean giving people something to do on the spur of the moment so they won't have time to worry about it or helping them forget a mistake and letting them try again. It is amazing how many people will grow and bloom under the supervision of a person who provides both confidence and opportunity.

## Failure to Enjoy Your Role as a Manager

There are many psychological rewards and perks to a supervisory position. If you don't isolate and enjoy them, you will render yourself less effective. For example, one of your rewards is more freedom. Enjoy this freedom by giving yourself work days filled with variety and special challenges to eliminate boredom. As you do this, remind yourself that your employees can afford to be negative or have occasional down days, but you can't. If you appear overburdened, washed-out, haggard and down, those who work for you will pick it up and the entire department will reflect your negative attitude. No matter how effective you are in other ways, if you don't stay positive and upbeat yourself, the productivity of your department will drop and your personal career will be damaged.

The very nature of the supervisor's job involves making mistakes. You will be no exception. With so many responsibilities you can't avoid it.

It is important then to avoid making the serious mistakes, the costly ones that damage both the department and your future as a supervisor.

**DISCUSSION QUESTIONS**

1. Why do many managers fail to receive the obvious signals (low productivity, complaints, and so forth) that they are not communicating with their employees?

2. Which supervisor would you prefer to work with? Supervisor A is a strong leader who knows when to get tough but at least you always know where you stand. Supervisor B is a more quiet and soft leader who is consistent and easy to work with but at times gets pushed around a little.

3. What can be done to help a manager who consistently stereotypes employees and thereby fails to encourage the development of their potential abilities to contribute?

# Intimidation

Ever since he took over the department, Supervisor Joe has been under subtle pressure to grant Mr. K a series of special favors. Most of the pressure has come from Mr. K himself who let Joe know from the beginning that he would support him in turn for certain freedoms to which he was entitled anyway because of his seniority and special knowledge. Some of the pressure, however has come from outside sources in the form of warnings. For example, one supervisor told Joe: "Treat Mr. K with kid gloves because he has powerful lines upstairs." So far Joe has gone along with the requests with growing resentment. It all came to a climax yesterday, however, when Mr. K asked if he could leave early Friday for personal reasons which he did not explain. Joe came back with a fast and emphatic no and walked away. Since then the following has happened. (1) Mr. K has been silent and sulky. (2) Mr. R came to Joe and complimented him on his stand in behalf of the other departmental employees. (3) Mr. X has reminded Joe that a previous supervisor resigned because Mr. K initiated a campaign to get rid of him.

Joe discusses the following options with you in confidence:

1. Stand pat and do nothing.

2. Protect flanks by going to Mr. Big and explaining the history of the problem and why you feel you must stand pat or lose the respect of the other employees. Tell him you want his complete support or he can have your resignation.

3. Back down by calling Mr. K into your office and telling him he is free to leave early Friday but must keep his special favor requests to an absolute minimum in the future.

4. Call Mr. K into your office and tell him firmly that you resent his going over your head to Mr. Big and talking outside the department and that you intend to stand by your decision and defend it all the way to the top.

Which option would you support? Why? What changes would you suggest to Joe in using it? What option (not on this list) might you propose?

# Converting Change into Opportunity

---

*After you give this chapter serious consideration, you should be able to convert most changes into career opportunities.*

---

Change is anything that happens in our environment that requires a human adjustment. When Alvin Toffler wrote *Future Shock* more than a decade ago, he predicted many drastic changes. Although these seemed unlikely or remote, some of them arrived ahead of time. The dramatic tempo has accelerated and the impact on the supervisor is greater today than anyone could have anticipated. The way you interpret and cope with such changes will have a measurable effect upon your future success.

**175**

Many times an individual hears about a pending change and promptly converts it into a dragon instead of an opportunity. You hear comments like these:

"This may force me into a nervous breakdown."

"What are they trying to do to me?"

"They are creating another monster."

Later, when such changes have arrived and there has been time to adjust, the dragon turns out to be a harmless caterpillar. The fear of change, psychologically magnified in the mind of the individual, has blown the change itself all out of proportion. Almost all employees adjust more easily than they realize. Sometimes, after a change has turned out to benefit everyone, the caterpillar turns into a beautiful butterfly.

How you cope with change as a supervisor will depend upon your attitude. Some people have the capacity to view change as opportunity; others reject even good changes with hostility. What is your attitude toward change? The following scale has been prepared to provide a few clues. Please rate yourself on all factors and compute your total score.

Not all changes are good or necessary. Resisting an ill-advised change can be a worthy mission that will protect and benefit your firm and your employees. But most changes are inevitable, and the sooner they are accepted by you as a supervisor, the better it will be for your employees. In spite of short-term adjustment disadvantages, many changes have long-term advantages that make the adjustment worthwhile. It will be your responsibility to communicate this situation to your employees when it occurs.

## Technological Changes Now in Their Infancy

Alvin Toffler, in his recent book *Third Wave,* develops the concept of the "electronic cottage." At some distant time, he predicts, most employees will work in their own homes, where electronic equipment will permit instant communication and directions from a central management source. Teachers will teach from their homes. Production workers will use sophisticated equipment to produce parts for a company miles away. Commuting to factories, skyscrapers, and other workplaces will be a thing of the past for many. People who live together will work together.

The electronic cottage may or may not become a reality, but many other changes will occur. Transportation, manufacturing, banking, medical, retailing, education, and government facilities are feeling the impact of change. As a management person, you will be caught in the middle. When sweeping changes come from above, it will be your responsibility to see that they are accepted by those who work below

## ATTITUDE-TOWARD-CHANGE SCALE

| | | | | | | |
|---|---|---|---|---|---|---|
| I view any change as an opportunity, not a threat. | 5 | 4 | 3 | 2 | 1 | I reject all change as a personal threat. |
| If my organization should introduce new equipment for me to use, I would be delighted. | 5 | 4 | 3 | 2 | 1 | If forced to learn how to use new equipment, I would be openly hostile. |
| A reorganization of my firm would be welcome; my flexibility would give me an advantage. | 5 | 4 | 3 | 2 | 1 | I would hate any form of reorganization; I like things stable and totally predictable. |
| I have an excellent superior, but a change would not bother me. | 5 | 4 | 3 | 2 | 1 | I have an excellent superior; a change would devastate me. |
| New work assignments and responsibilities motivate me. | 5 | 4 | 3 | 2 | 1 | New work assignments and responsibilities demotivate me. |
| All of the social and political changes taking place today are exciting to me. | 5 | 4 | 3 | 2 | 1 | I wish I had lived a hundred years ago. |
| Predictability is dull. | 5 | 4 | 3 | 2 | 1 | Predictability is beautiful. |
| The possibility of a career change intrigues me. | 5 | 4 | 3 | 2 | 1 | The possibility of a career change deflates me. |
| I have confidence I can quickly change my behavioral patterns to fit any contingency. | 5 | 4 | 3 | 2 | 1 | In all honesty, it is almost impossible for me to change my behavioral patterns. |
| I can change my career and lifestyle goals quickly. | 5 | 4 | 3 | 2 | 1 | My career goals and values are bedded in cement. |

TOTAL [      ]

If you rated yourself above 25, you appear to have a positive, flexible attitude toward change. You should be able to handle future changes effectively. If you rated yourself below 25, you have less flexibility than you may need to cope well with future changes.

you. Even more critical, you will need to teach employees new techniques and procedures so that change can take place. Wherever you work as a supervisor, technological change will make your role more difficult. You can view these changes as opportunities to prepare yourself for a higher position, or you can take a negative view and eliminate yourself from the race.

When May heard that her savings and loan firm would adopt a more sophisticated computer system, her first reaction was negative. As an operations officer, she knew the change would throw substantial new responsibility upon her. She would have to undergo additional training that would be difficult. Besides learning new skills, she would spend many hours of additional time helping her nine employees adjust. At first she even considered changing her career. But after talking things over with a close friend, she decided to turn the announcement into an opportunity. She said to herself, "If computers are going to dominate this industry, then I am going to dominate computers so that I can use my skills to increase my upward mobility." She promptly enrolled an Institute of Financial Education course that would improve her skills with computers. She also enrolled in a general course in data processing at a local college, and she welcomed all the information provided by the computer firm. May was determined to take advantage of change to improve her own future. Her superiors were quick to recognize her positive attitude toward changes over which they, too, had little control.

## Organizations Change to Survive

There was a time in the United States when a supervisor felt lucky to work for a stable, predictable corporation. The supervisor could anticipate security and upward mobility within the framework of a single, large organization. The corporate womb was a safe, comfortable place to be. As a first-line supervisor, you could blueprint a career path to the top with confidence. You knew, at least to some extent, what was ahead.

Today, the supervisor should feel lucky if he or she works for an organization that is sufficiently flexible to adjust to changes and survive. Organizations who are too slow to adjust will be left behind. Supervisors and employees who belong to such organizations will find themselves unemployed.

Changes are hitting firms of all sizes with increasing magnitude. Mergers, takeovers, and staff reductions are in the headlines. You should not infer that the organization you are currently working for is so vulnerable to change that it may turn belly-up. But if your organization is not adaptable enough to survive, your job may disappear. Your attitude should be, "I'm lucky that the management of my organization is flexible enough to keep the organization alive and changing." It should *not* be, "I hope my organization can resist change and stay the way it is."

As a supervisor, you are in a key role to help your organization survive and prosper. You will need to be flexible enough to reorganize your department, accept new technology and assignments, and, most of all, assist your employees in their adjustment.

Doug couldn't understand why his firm needed to make changes. As a result he resisted what few changes were made and refused to learn new techniques that were revolutionizing his particular career area. Because of inflexible, shortsighted management, his firm went into bankruptcy, and Doug was left out on a limb. His failure to learn new techniques left him unprepared for a similar job with another firm. He had contributed to the demise of his organization and permitted himself to become obsolete in his career specialty.

The United States work force has been changing rapidly during the last ten years. It is becoming multicultural and multilingual. Women are moving into all occupations and making faster progress up executive ladders. Blacks, Hispanics, and Orientals are improving their skills and earning greater upward mobility. First-generation workers from foreign cultures are arriving and making adjustments to the work force. The new work force is a challenge to the front-line supervisor because it is he or she who must work with all individuals on a personal, one-to-one basis.

**The Work Force Changes**

Ten years ago Herbert had twenty employees in his department: seventeen white males, two white females, and one black male. Today, thanks to his human-relations skills, productivity is higher with only sixteen employees. The composition is as follows: five white females, four white males, two black males, two Orientals, one black female, one Hispanic male, and one Hispanic female. Herbert takes pride in the cultural mix of his department. From the start, he accepted the change as a personal challenge and enjoyed helping the few remaining senior employees in his department to adjust.

*Supervisor's Survival Kit* is designed to prevent burnout. The "manage yourself" chapters have been written to help you do the best possible job and still protect your emotional health. Supervisors who establish realistic goals, maintain comfortable priorities, and manage their time are in a position to balance their careers with their personal lifestyles. This balance helps prevent burnout when things are stable. When major changes occur—they always introduce more stress—the supervisor is prepared for temporary adjustments until career and home are again properly balanced. A balanced, happy, activity-centered, relaxing "home life" is the best insurance against stress generated in the workplace.

**Management Burnout**

Employee stress comes from many sources, such as work overload, role conflicts, oversupervision, ambiguity, and insecurity. Although you want to protect your employees from such pressures, you cannot provide a 100 percent stress-free work environment. In fact, mild stress stimulates greater productivity. Some work environments such as the media, advertising, and political activity have built-in stress situations. The way you handle change in your department, however, can eliminate a great deal of harmful stress that might injure employees and eat away at productivity standards.

**Change as a Source of Stress**

To convert dragons into caterpillars, you will want to portray such changes as opportunities for growth instead of problems to overcome. You will want to communicate such changes in a nonthreatening way as far in advance as possible so that employees have time to adjust. You will also want to explain why such changes are necessary.

**Summary**    As you accomplish these goals, consider the following suggestions.

*Turn change into opportunity for yourself.*    When it comes to change, it doesn't hurt to think of yourself first because if you don't succeed, those working for you will be left unprepared. It is bad enough to work for a supervisor who is negative about change; it is even worse to work for one who neglects to prepare you for the future.

*Communicate the advantages of change.*    Tell your staff that changing now may save their jobs later. Relate to them that the way to protect their retirement pensions in the future is to change to greater profitability now. Do this individually, in staff meetings, and during formal appraisal periods. Prepare your people to anticipate change and learn to roll with the punches. You will be doing them an immense favor.

*Follow up with advanced, hands-on training.*    Frequently highly capable persons take their skills with them into a new company or community only to discover their competencies are obsolete. Do not let this happen to your staff. Provide them with the kind of training they need to stay up with career demands where they are or where they move in the future. Allowing your staff to rest on their career laurels is doing them a disservice.

When one accepts the premise that change is inevitable, then it is possible to take pride in being able to cope with change effectively. Anything you can do to help your employees experience this pride will make you a superior supervisor.

**DISCUSSION QUESTIONS**

1. Can all changes be converted into opportunities? Defend your answer through examples.

2. What can supervisors do to minimize stress within themselves? Evaluate such possibilities as physical exercise and meditation.

3. Would you agree that change is the primary source of stress in our society?

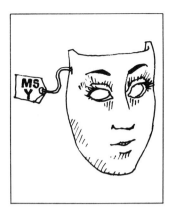

# Change

## Objective

To provide the supervisor both insights and techniques to help a negative mature worker accept change.

## Problem

Ms. Y is concerned about an employee, Mrs. B. During more than twenty years with the organization, Mrs. B was highly productive. For the last year, however, she has been negative to both co-workers and customers. Every time a change is mandated by top management, Mrs. B becomes more vocal and more negative. Now co-workers are complaining and customers are turning to competitors. In addition, Mrs. B's inflexible attitude toward change is hurting the productivity of everyone who works with her. Ms. Y agrees that something must be done. The organization has a nontermination policy for employees in Mrs. B's category.

## Procedure

The seminar, workshop, or classroom is divided into small groups of four or five. Each group selects its own chairperson. The group then develops a counseling strategy that will help Mrs. B to cope with change and return to her previous positive attitude and high productivity.

The strategy should include: (1) counseling techniques, either directive or nondirective, (2) a decision whether the Mutual Reward Theory (MRT) would be effective, (3) the number of sessions recommended, and (4) choice of superiors who will be involved.

**181**

Give each group at least twenty minutes to develop strategy, followed by an opportunity to present its conclusions to the class or seminar.

**Postgame Discussion**

Compare the strategies presented and evaluate their probable effectiveness in improving Mrs. B's attitude.

# Having a Plan B

*This chapter should convince you that it would be smart for you develop a Plan B for yourself.*

If you are happy and effective as a front-line supervisor, chances are excellent you will eventually aspire to further upward mobility. Success at one level has a way of pushing an individual toward a higher level for many reasons, including the prospect of additional financial rewards, greater ego satisfaction, and the opportunity to test one's leadership ability in more demanding situations.

What about you? Would you like to use your first supervisory position as a springboard? Do you have ambitions to climb the management ladder? If so, this chapter will have special meaning for you because it is designed to take you above and beyond the realm of operating a

**183**

successful department. You, too, can reach the upper levels of management by building strong working relationships with other supervisors and executives as well; you can play the management game with experienced professionals in a way that will help you contribute both to the growth of the organization and yourself. Sound interesting? Here is the way Bob Spencer sizes up the situation.

Even with a four-year degree in business administration, it took me more than two years to become the kind of frontline supervisor I wanted to be. I had more to learn than I suspected when I started out. Once I had everything under control, however, I became intrigued with taking the next step. I then discovered a whole new dimension of communications, human relations, decision making, and management know-how. The first-line supervisor is a babe in the woods compared to the experienced middle manager. I suddenly realized I had just started to learn what I would eventually need to know to move up to more competitive middle management. It appeared far more demanding than I had expected, but I decided to start preparing myself. I had made the first step successfully, so why stop? Besides, I had a feeling that if I didn't keep preparing for something bigger, I might lose interest in what I already had. I work for a rather high-powered organization and if you stand still too long, others often pass you up.

Do you agree with Bob? Do you feel it might be wise to prepare for a more demanding role in management? If so, most executives would agree that you must start playing the management game from your present position as a front-line supervisor. To do this you might consider making the following moves now.

**Making Yourself Visible**

*Make yourself visible.*   To make yourself visible, you must be seen and talked about by management people above you. You must be noticed. There are many ways to do this.

- Speaking up (sometimes critically) in staff meetings.
- Turning in written suggestions through channels.
- Making appointments with upper management people to ask questions but always going through channels.
- Being seen around the facility—in the cafeteria, personnel office, and other places.
- Participating in organizational events or recreational activities.
- Taking advantage of lunch to meet other people.

Of course, the best way to be visible is to do a good job and get recognition from doing it. In fact, it may be more important to be visible silently rather than physically or verbally. There is also the danger of being visible in a negative way. Some supervisors become too aggressive and play the management game too forcefully, hurting instead of helping their personal progress.

*Show strength from your present position.*    If you are to move upward toward executive management, you must occasionally stand pat on your own two feet and refuse to be pushed around. This may mean quietly standing up to your superior and other management people when you know you are right and have all the facts to document your case or holding your own in controversy over the role of your department; it may mean fighting back in an acceptable way when someone tries to invade your area of responsibility. You can't build a strong reputation as a leader if you always back down under pressure. When you know you are right, stand up for your ideas. This is the best way to win the respect of some top managers.

*Always defend and protect your employees to outsiders.*    You cannot move up the executive ladder without the enthusiastic support and loyalty of the employees in your department. You earn some of this loyalty when you go to bat for them with outsiders. This way you keep departmental problems inside the department where they belong. The easiest way to destroy a good departmental image is to air dirty laundry with outsiders. Your employees are free to do this any time they wish. However, if you defend and protect them, they will probably do the same for you.

*Do your homework.*    If you keep your department in top shape at all times, you will not be vulnerable to those who may wish to stop your personal progress. Some extremely ambitious supervisors spend so much time playing management politics that they neglect their department and defeat themselves. You can afford to work on outside communications only when your department is completely under control. You can make outside moves only when you are safe from attack yourself.

*Stand firm with other supervisors.*    You will need the support of other supervisors if you hope to join middle management because in many cases you will be supervising them following your promotion.

Sound, healthy relationships with other supervisors can be developed, but it is naive to expect them all to be open and supportive. You are their competitor, so some may use devious tactics to undermine you, try to out maneuver you to gain something you both want, or even try to trick you into a poor move that will give them an advantage. Of course, most will be aboveboard and easy to work with. Even when other competitors use unfair tactics, your best move is to win their respect without resorting to the same methods. Protect yourself and your department while maintaining your personal standards and belief in human relations principles. Be tough in defending what you feel is right, but avoid revenge or vindictiveness. Such conduct will only destroy the reputation you are attempting to build.

*Be a team player in staff meetings.*   The staff meeting is the perfect setting to make either good or bad impressions, so it will be a challenge to get the right kind of reactions from other management people in this environment. Here are some suggestions that might help. (1) Don't hesitate to speak up when you really have something to say, but don't overdo it. Overtalking and underlistening is a serious malady. (2) Make critical contributions now and then even if it is something your own manager doesn't want to hear. In short, say what you really believe—don't just accommodate the group. (3) When you do say something, be brief and stick to the topic at hand. (4) Support others enthusiastically if you agree with them. This is a sound way to build relationships with other supervisors. (5) If you lose interest in a staff meeting that is dragging, try not to show it. Sometimes you can tolerate it by arranging your priorities, thinking about a problem, or some other mental activity so long as you don't miss anything vital. (6) Never show personal hostility in a staff meeting.

*Read and study.*   The supervisor who stops reading is locking the doors to opportunity and throwing the key away. This includes reading company brochures, bulletins, reports, research papers, as well as outside articles and books on management techniques. The ambitious supervisor must keep informed on company matters and prevailing management practices or, sooner or later, he or she will be passed by.

*Look as though you are ready.*   It should go without saying that a junior manager on the way up must look ready. He or she should project an image of confidence, demonstrate leadership, stay constantly organized, and handle problems with finesse. In short, you should communicate upwards—through your leadership style—a readiness factor that shows you are stronger than your competition.

There are two different routes you can take to reach the top: on the straight-line route you climb the ladder of your present organization; on the zigzag route, you change employers.

The choice you make is critical and should involve a careful study of your own personality, values, and lifestyles.

## The Straight Line to the Top

If you are currently a supervisor for a sizable organization you respect, you may prefer to work your way to the top within the framework of this same firm. You might say to yourself, "This is a strong organization with a bright future, and I prefer to settle in and build my career without looking outside for better opportunities." The straight line is a comfortable pattern to take. It permits you to enjoy your work, build long-term working relationships, and feel secure without constantly working to build outside contacts. It also permits you to stay in one geographical location without frequent moves. You can enjoy staying in the same home, permitting your children to mature in the same school system, and generally establishing your roots in the community of your choice. In the past most top executives followed this pattern to the top.

There are, however, three precautions you should take. First, you must make certain that the organization you select has future growth potential and can survive under changing conditions. Second, you must stay self-motivated. When ambitious supervisors who accept this strategy become complacent, management is forced to go outside to fill top leadership roles. Third, you must assertively communicate to management that you are capable, loyal, creative, and dependable, and because of these characteristics, you deserve the next promotion available. You cannot assume management will recognize your accomplishments.

The alternative to the straight-line approach is zigzagging your way to the top by moving from one organization to another—always making a major contribution as you go. The zigzag pattern takes more energy, involves more risk, and requires greater flexibility. Those who make this pattern work (scramblers) usually stay with one firm a minimum of two years. They are highly motivated and constantly learn new ideas to take with them as they travel on. They spend a great deal of time making contacts. These individuals talk about their "Plan B's." A Plan B is a well devised strategy that permits the individual to move quickly to a new firm if promotional opportunities begin to fade at home. While most supervisors spend all their energy on their jobs, scramblers work hard to contribute where they are but exert extra energy to locate better opportunities elsewhere—they put their personal careers ahead of the organization. Being more assertive in promoting themselves, they do not always play by traditional rules.

**The Zigzag Pattern**

Most observers agree that the zigzag route will take a person to the top faster, but it has its disadvantages. First, the individual must occasionally uproot his or her family to make a geographical move. Second, a person needs more talent and energy to make it work. Third, if not careful, the individual may create resentment among fellow-workers—which can, in turn, force the person to make a move more quickly.

Although the zigzag route is attractive in many respects, not everyone can make it work. The scrambler is a person with high mentality, great energy, and a willingness to take risks. Although moving from one work environment to another is demanding, there is some evidence that it builds better leadership. The individual has to make more adjustments and more decisions. The very act of moving seems to enhance the individual's personal growth.

If you want upward mobility, your master plan should take into consideration the advantages and disadvantages of both patterns. The Scrambler-Stabilizer Scale will assist you in this undertaking. Assume

SCRAMBLER-STABILIZER SCALE

Please circle a number to rate yourself honestly on a scale from 1 to 5.

| | | | | | | |
|---|---|---|---|---|---|---|
| I will always welcome any geographic move that enhances my career. | 5 | 4 | 3 | 2 | 1 | I would turn down any job opportunity that involves moving. |
| Zigzagging from one firm to another would be intriguing to me. | 5 | 4 | 3 | 2 | 1 | I hate the process of adjusting to new work environments. |
| My career is first; my personal lifestyle is second. | 5 | 4 | 3 | 2 | 1 | My personal lifestyle is first; my career is second. |
| Getting to the top through zigzagging is more of a challenge. | 5 | 4 | 3 | 2 | 1 | Getting to the top in one organization is more of a challenge. |
| I am willing to take risks even though I might lose my job. | 5 | 4 | 3 | 2 | 1 | I will not take any risks that puts my job in jeopardy. |
| My ultimate loyalty is only to myself and my career. | 5 | 4 | 3 | 2 | 1 | I am 100 percent loyal to my organization. |
| I do not intend to follow traditional rules in order to get to the top. | 5 | 4 | 3 | 2 | 1 | I intend to follow traditional rules to the fullest extent. |
| I enjoy the job-seeking process, especially interviews. | 5 | 4 | 3 | 2 | 1 | I hate the job-seeking process, especially interviews. |
| I am willing to spend the extra energy to have a plan B ready and waiting. | 5 | 4 | 3 | 2 | 1 | I do not bother with a plan B. I devote my energy to my firm and my job. |
| It would not bother me in the least if I lost my job tomorrow. | 5 | 4 | 3 | 2 | 1 | I would be devastated if I lost my job tomorrow. |

TOTAL ☐

If you rated yourself 25 or higher, you should give the zigzagging pattern (scrambling) careful consideration.  If you rated yourself under 25, the straight-line pattern appears to be a better choice for you.

that you are highly ambitious and capable of excelling in higher leadership roles. Which pattern fits your personality and values?

## The Importance of a Plan B

Although scramblers *must* design and implement a Plan B if they intend to zigzag their way to the top, stabilizers can also benefit from a Plan B for the following reasons.

(1) As discussed in Chapter 18, mergers, takeovers, and highly volatile market conditions may render your position (or even your employer) obsolete. Without a Plan B you can, through no fault of your own, be left high and dry.

(2) Having a Plan B will help keep you informed about what is going on in the marketplace and thus contribute to your professional growth *where you are*. For example, in forming a Plan B, you may discover you need to return to school to upgrade your competencies. The new skills will help your present firm.

(3) A Plan B can help keep you motivated. Knowing you are capable of building a career elsewhere can make you feel better where you are currently employed. You will feel more secure. You will be more inclined to speak up and contribute more without fear. If you are doing an excellent job and your superior discovers you have a Plan B, she or he may appreciate you more.

Stabilizers can benefit from a Plan B without ever exercising it.

**Networking**

All scramblers and most stabilizers believe in some form of networking. Networking is the practice of actively seeking out and building relationships with colleagues inside and outside your firm—significant people who can keep you informed and, if necessary, come to your aid at a later date. If sound, mutually rewarding relationships are built, such networks can provide you with a *career support system*. That is, an inner circle of colleagues who can help you professionally in many ways.

Network inner circles can include co-workers and superiors in the same company, counterparts in competitive organizations, trade association friends you may see only at conventions, college professors you have maintained relationships with, and many others. Three professionals who endorse the system comment:

''I think the word networking is over-used but the idea of building relationships with other professionals so you can experience greater personal approach is an excellent idea.''

''I have made two beneficial career changes in the last five years—in each instance I found my new job through a network contact.''

''My career has been enhanced through membership in my local chapter of the Financial Institute. Should I seek a new career opportunity, I would contact a few key chapter members first.''

**DISCUSSION QUESTIONS**

1. How, in your opinion, can ambitious stabilizers compete more successfully with talented scramblers within the same organization?

2. Do you agree with the author that moving from one organization (environment) to another is a good way to improve one's leadership ability?

3. Should stabilizers develop Plan B's even if they have no intention of leaving their firms?

# Decision

Eric is thirty years old and an engineer for a giant utility. Commuting daily from the suburbs to a central city headquarters, he arrives early but refuses to work beyond 4:30 P.M. except in emergencies. Eric puts his lifestyle first and clearly separates work from his private life. He is highly family- and church-oriented.

Management believes that Eric is talented, ethical and patient enough to play the corporate game. Eric's co-workers know he is extremely ambitious and growing increasingly impatient. Eric is usually self-motivated, but now things are beginning to drag. He has the impression management is keeping him in an unnecessary holding pattern, possibly because of a prior image resulting from some unfortunate experiences early in his career. The solution is aggravated now because management is pouring responsibility upon Eric without giving him additional recognition. He senses that they view him as "good old dependable Eric."

Eric prefers the straight-line pattern to the top because it gives his family stability and permits him to maintain his present church connections. He is, however, considering the zigzag pattern. Other firms would recognize his skills and experience, and a new job in a new environment would provide greater personal growth. Eric freely admits that he is in conflict between the two upward mobility patterns.

What advice would you give Eric? Upon what values should he base his decision? Can Eric take the zigzag path without sacrificing family values?

# Put More Leadership into Your Style

*If you give this chapter a chance, you will become a stronger, more effective leader.*

Leadership is not a gift awarded to some and denied to others. No magic is involved, and no special personality or unusual charisma is required. Most individuals who truly wish to become leaders can develop leadership ability.

Leadership is stepping out in front of others with confidence, taking charge, and earning the support of followers.

A perceptive observer can sense the presence of strong leadership. The group under observation is pulling together in an organized, efficient manner. Members show enthusiasm and a sense of direction. There

**191**

is an absence of tension because everybody expects to benefit from the group's activity. Everybody supports the leader because of respect that the leader has earned.

**Your Opportunity to Become a Leader**

For most workers the leadership-building process starts when they become supervisors. Some may get a head start through experience as club officers, team captains, chairpersons, and officers in trade or volunteer organizations, but supervisory jobs are the primary leadership builders.

It is possible to be a good supervisor without being a good leader, but it is impossible to be a good leader without being a good supervisor or manager. Those who become leaders without first becoming supervisors must ultimately learn management skills such as setting priorities, learning to delegate, and other principles and techniques covered in this book. They must do this to free themselves to lead. Many supervisors become so bogged down with administrative details they do not have time to put more leadership into their styles.

*Your leadership style should reflect your personality.* Although you can learn about leadership from others by using them as models, you must nevertheless create your own style, a style that reflects your personality, supervisory approach, and the kind of leader you want to be. You can learn a lot about leadership by observing your superiors, but you should feel free to adapt or reject their methods to your own highly individualized style.

In building your own leadership style, it is important that you identify your strong personal characteristics and strengthen them. Your style is an extension of these characteristics. When you emphasize a unique trait, say a strong, powerful voice, you are building a style that causes you to stand out from others. It is vital, however, that you channel your special characteristics into certain foundations that reflect strong leadership.

**A Leadership Formula**

Based upon over sixty interviews with successful leaders in a wide variety of roles, the leadership pyramid below was developed.* The formula projects the five foundations upon which those interviewed built their own leadership styles. Your challenge is to strengthen your strong and develop your weaker personality traits to fit into these foundations. In doing this you will automatically put more leadership into your supervisory style.

---

*Since submitting the manuscript for the third edition of *Supervisor's Survival Kit* in 1982, Elwood Chapman has written a separate publication with the same title as this chapter—*Put More Leadership Into Your Style.* The leadership formula, briefly presented here, is fully developed in this 200 page effort. For further information write: Science Research Associates, Inc., College and Vocational Studies, 155 North Wacker Drive, Chicago, Illinois 60606.

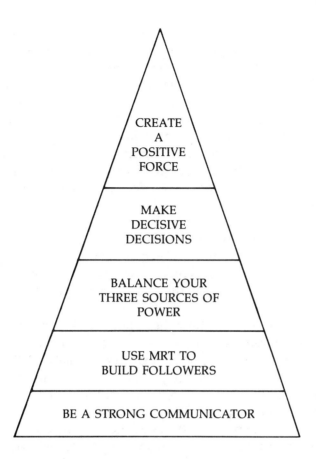

CREATE
A
POSITIVE
FORCE

MAKE
DECISIVE
DECISIONS

BALANCE YOUR
THREE SOURCES OF
POWER

USE MRT TO
BUILD FOLLOWERS

BE A STRONG COMMUNICATOR

Starting at the base of the pyramid, your first step in putting more leadership into your style is to become a more dynamic communicator. Followers like their leaders to speak with authority. They want them to *sound* like leaders.

**Be A Strong Communicator**

Dixie was an outstanding supervisor but she was so soft-spoken in her approach to group meetings and counseling that those in her department became impatient. Some even went so far as to say she was "too nice." Dixie's superior and mentor, a woman with a strong, commanding voice, suggested that Dixie take a course in public speaking. Dixie rejected the idea but took the suggestion to mean that she should demonstrate more leadership through her voice. She started to exercise more control through her voice in both private counseling and group sessions. Within three months her superior complimented her on the change and asked what grade she had received in her public speaking course. "I didn't take one," Dixie replied. "I used you as a model and made the changes myself."

Of course, speaking with confidence is only one part of your communications system. A good communications system is a planned program of daily two-way communications to keep those who work for you informed. An effective communication system can include all or part of the following: daily personal contact with workers on the site, a bulletin board where both supervisor and employee can leave messages that will be picked up daily, regular group staff meetings, informal communications during break periods, use of in-house communications media (bulletins, house organs), telephone calls, distribution of personal notes, voluntary or designed counseling sessions. Each leader must design and maintain a system appropriate to the work environment. It must be a two-way system that works on a daily basis. A breakdown in the communications system is as serious as a breakdown of production equipment.

Why is such a system so important?

It is essential to keep everyone informed and prevent misunderstandings. Silence—not knowing what is going on—destroys morale. When workers are involved in decisions, or at least informed, they can cope with changes. Being left out in the cold develops hostility that can even lead to mutiny in extreme cases.

Employees need to know how they are doing as individuals and how their contribution relates to departmental goals. Knowing this provides job security and reassurance, which many desperately need almost daily. When employees know where they stand, they relax and produce more. Within the security of the group, they feel they belong. A good communications system keeps workers from feeling neglected, misinterpreting, or becoming suspicious. It keeps them involved.

Leaders need the ideas that can come only from their followers. They must listen to suggestions and then provide credit to those who make them. A good leader discovers problems and solves them before they become disruptive. The only way to make such discoveries is through a sound, two-way communications system that brings problems to the attention of the leader. Weak and ineffective leaders usually discover problems too late. A leader with a strong, commanding voice who does not have a two-way communications system eventually loses the respect of followers. A leader with an authoritative voice *and* a well-maintained communications system has the winning combination.

**Use MRT To Build Followers**   The best way to create enthusiastic followers (foundation number 2 in the leadership pyramid) is to put the Mutual Reward Theory (MRT) to work with more intensity. The supervisor (leader) and employee (follower) can easily reward each other. The supervisor can provide an enjoyable, consistent work environment, opportunity to learn, and freedom to operate without being stifled. The employee, on the other hand, can provide productivity, dependability, and freedom from unnecessary problems. There is a natural *reward exchange* between a supervisor and an employee, and rewards can be considered tradeoffs.

The supervisor who provides unusual opportunities for self-improvement, for example, may gain an increase in productivity in return. Mutual rewards strengthen the relationship—and enhance the image of the leader. Both people are coming out ahead and they know it.

Leadership, in a sense, is an impression in the mind of the follower. If the needs of the worker are satisfied, the supervisor appears to be a good leader; if the needs are not satisfied, then the worker feels thwarted and neglected and has a poor image of the supervisor. And when workers produce at high levels because their needs are amply satisfied, they convert their supervisors into leaders in the view of upper management. The workers push their supervisor up the management ladder.

> When Ralph was first introduced to MRT he dismissed it as nothing more than the old truism, "You scratch my back and I'll scratch yours." But later, after a discussion with a superior he respected, he decided to try it. As a supervisor, he discovered that he could furnish many rewards he had previously neglected. When he sat down with an employee and openly discussed the "reward exchange" that was possible between them, a better relationship and higher productivity resulted. In six months time Ralph had progressed from a good supervisor and average leader to a better supervisor and a good leader. Through the application of MRT he had put more leadership into his style.

**Balance Your Three Sources Of Power**

As a supervisor, you have three basic sources of power to draw upon to establish your reputation as a leader. First is the power that comes from your role as a supervisor. You are in charge of those in your department, and this responsibility gives you authority to require certain behavior from your workers. You must be careful, however, not to overwork this source of power. Second, you have power because of your knowledge. Your followers respect you because they recognize that you know more than they do. You have the skills and know-how that make you a good supervisor, and you use your knowledge to help your followers. This source of leadership power is seldom overworked. Third, you have the power of your own personality. You can influence your followers through the force of your own person. You don't want to come on too strong, but you must accept the role of supervisor and leader and show confidence in yourself as you take various actions and make decisions.

You should draw carefully from the power bank composed of your role position, knowledge, and personality, but you should not hesitate to draw from it when necessary. Without a firm and consistent discipline line a department cannot reach productivity goals. When such goals are not reached, everyone suffers. Utilizing your power sources in a sensitive, balanced manner may be the best way to put more leadership into your style.

Janice knew she had replaced an authoritarian manager. After careful consideration she decided she could gain greater productivity from the nine office workers in her department if she relied primarily on her knowledge power and soft-peddled her role and personality power. Janice said to herself: "If I can teach them more about the automated equipment and increase their competencies, they will sense my knowledge power and little else will be necessary. Things progressed in a satisfactory manner for some time, but slowly her employees began to slow down and take advantage of her. Janice had made the classic mistake of depending upon one source of power. She quickly fell back on her role power by demonstrating her strength as a firm, no-nonsense supervisor. In addition, Janice became a stronger personality—using her special characteristics (warm voice, persuasive manner, etc.) to project more leadership. It took only a few weeks to get back to higher productivity and a more cohesive department.

**Make Decisive Decisions**

Although you will eventually be judged upon the quality of your decisions and your long-term record, the way you announce your decision is important. A good decision forcefully announced communicates the presence of leadership. In fact, a poor decision forcefully announced communicates the presence of leadership. A poor decision timidly announced communicates the absence of leadership. Even an excellent decision that is announced in a wishy-washy manner turns out to be weak if it is not accepted and put into operation by followers.

From the viewpoint of followers, leadership is decisiveness. A strong leader carefully analyzes the problem and then chooses one direction or the other with confidence. Supervisors who straddle the fence and push problems under the carpet do not communicate strong leadership.

Kenneth had spent all afternoon evaluating the new advertising campaign. He had seen all the layouts and considered their probable impact on sales and on the corporate image. He was not satisfied with the program, but there was no time to develop a better proposal. He decided to support the advertising staff, accept their plan, and do everything in his power to make it work. He called in the staff and complimented them on their proposal. Then he wrote a short, enthusiastic article about the campaign for the in-house bulletin. In every possible way he communicated the idea that the right decision had been made. As it turned out, the advertising program was moderately successful, primarily because of the enthusiasm behind it. Equally important to Kenneth, he had protected his leadership image. In fact, he was never criticized because the program's success was only moderate. His staff and other followers continued to support his leadership.

Leaders who expect to bat a thousand in making sound decisions will, of course, fall short of their expectations. But those who are afraid to make any decisions are doomed to failure. As one supervisor stated, "You can't expect to win 'em all, but you can win often enough to keep your workers' respect. And a decision made with confidence has a better chance of success because your employees will try to make it work. When you're indecisive, you only get into trouble.''

Workers often interpret your decisions from a highly personal point of view. ''Does the decision give me more or less job security? Will it enhance my career progress or slow it down?'' Employees like decisions that are good for themselves as well as the organization. The skillful leader makes sure that employees see how they can benefit from whatever is best for the organization.

Decisions that encompass too many compromises do little for the supervisor's leadership image. Those that are based upon facts and made with gusto are usually well received. A good decision-maker inspires respect. Such a leader makes employees feel they are in good hands. The department is making progress and headed in the right direction.

At the top of the leadership pyramid, and to some experts, the most important foundation, is becoming a positive force. Being a positive force as a supervisor is more than staying friendly, upbeat, and positive—it is generating a stream of activities that moves a department in the direction where all will benefit. A positive force (leader) sends out positive waves that stir followers up—motivate—remove obstacles—and lead to constructive action. It is, in effect, a form of energy. Although a positive force stems from a leader's positive attitude, it is the ability to create a group psychology that picks up the momentum. When this happens, it is difficult for a employee to stand on the sidelines and not be drawn into it.

**Create A Positive Force**

> When Bernie took over as supervisor, lassitude prevailed. The staff was lethargic and difficult to motivate. Within six weeks the opposite was true. Employees were full of energy and anxious to contribute. How did Bernie turn things around? He put the first four foundations of the leadership pyramid into operation and topped them off by setting loose a moving force from his own energy source and personality. Bernie stirred things up through his own activity—he seemed to be everywhere at the same time. Through a new wave of delegating, he saw that every staff member had more to do and received more satisfaction from doing it. He stayed in constant communication with staff members, creating and releasing their talents. Using his personality power, he created laughter where previously there was silence. Like a centrifugal force, Bernie expressed his leadership by being in the center of things but at the same time encouraging others to demonstrate their own talents in new directions.

By carrying out the responsibilities of a supervisor as outlined in this book, you will automatically develop a certain amount of leadership. But don't stop there. Use your personality power—and the leadership pyramid— to put more leadership into your supervisory style. More than anything else you can do, this approach will set you apart from other supervisors and move you into higher management positions.

**DISCUSSION QUESTIONS**

1. Do you agree with the statement that it is possible to be a good manager without being a leader? Explain fully.

2. Do you feel that most supervisors would be more successful if they put additional leadership into their style?

3. Do you feel that the leadership formula is complete? What, if anything, should be added?

---

A 30-minute film *Put More Leadership Into Your Style* is now available from Barr Films, 3490 E. Foothill Blvd., P.O. Box 5667, Pasadena, California 91107 (213) 681-6978.

# Trade-Offs

## Objective

To give participants practice in the application of the Mutual Reward Theory.

## Problem

Mr. Big wants Supervisor Joe to put more leadership into his style. He feels that Joe must first learn how to make MRT work.

## Procedure

All nonmanagement players (five roles) select from the list below what they feel are the ten most important employee needs that Joe should provide. In a separate small group those assigned to the four management roles will list what rewards they would expect if they satisfied those needs. (Such a list should include high productivity and loyalty, for example.) Those not playing roles should be assigned to small groups and asked to write their own lists—one for employee needs and one for management rewards. After 20 minutes, both employee and management groups will write their lists on the board, and the instructor will attempt to get a trade-off between the two groups. When both groups agree that they will provide the rewards listed on the board (no specific number), the game has been completed.

## Postgame Discussion

Consider how Supervisor Joe might maintain an even exchange and what MRT might do to improve his role as a leader.

### EMPLOYEE NEEDS

Opportunity for self-improvement on the job
Freedom from close supervision
Ample time for socializing
Freedom to take breaks without following a schedule
Opportunity to express self in group situations
Chance to have some "fun times" on the job
Opportunity to rotate among different jobs
Credit for accomplishments
Involvement in the decision-making process
Knowing what is going on
Opportunity to use limited work time for personal business
Chance to learn supervisor's job
Opportunity to talk about personal problems

**199**

Chance to extend coffee and lunch breaks without asking permission
Opportunity to use telephone for (local) personal calls
Assurance that job is secure
Having a supervisor who is accessible
Knowing about changes in advance
Selecting one's own vacation schedule
Learning new things from one's supervisor

# Role Profiles For Cases and Mini-Games

Identifying with the nine profiles that follow will help make the cases in *Supervisor's Survival Kit* more realistic and enjoyable. The same is true of the Mini-Games. If you have the opportunity to play a role in a Mini-Game (group situation), you will be expected to make decisions from the view-point of the character you portray. For example, if you are given the role of Mr. Big, you will attempt to act in a way you feel a top-management person with his personality would act.

The chart gives you the power positions of each individual in our hypothetical organization. The more you study and identify with these roles, the more intriguing will be the Case Studies and Mini-Games.

**Mini-Games: The Organization and the Players**

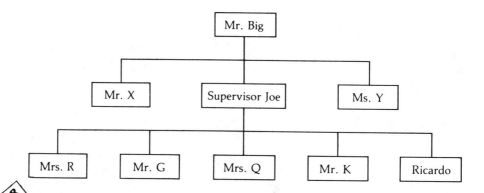

```
                        ┌──────────┐
                        │  Mr. Big │
                        └──────────┘
            ┌────────────────┼────────────────┐
       ┌────────┐     ┌──────────────┐    ┌────────┐
       │ Mr. X  │     │ Supervisor Joe│    │ Ms. Y  │
       └────────┘     └──────────────┘    └────────┘
        ┌──────────┬──────────┼──────────┬──────────┐
   ┌────────┐ ┌────────┐ ┌────────┐ ┌────────┐ ┌─────────┐
   │ Mrs. R │ │ Mr. G  │ │ Mrs. Q │ │ Mr. K  │ │ Ricardo │
   └────────┘ └────────┘ └────────┘ └────────┘ └─────────┘
```

As Mr. Big you occupy the number-one power role. You consider yourself a professional manager and a strong leader. Your superiors recognize you as ambitious, efficient, and a good listener. You are a stabilizer (as opposed to a scrambler*) in that you intend to stay with your present organization and take a straight line to the top. You measure your people on productivity not personality; because you are good at setting priorities and managing your own time, you expect the same efficiency from others; you maintain a clear and firm discipline line. You sense you are an excellent model for supervisors who report to you.

You feel very fortunate to be in your present position at the age of thirty-five. You credit your rise in the company to your four-year college degree in business management, your leadership qualities and your willingness to work harder than others. You are married and have three children You are a runner and have participated in three marathons. You spend a great deal of time at home reading management books and periodicals because you want to be known as a supervisor's supervisor.

You like Supervisor Joe as a person, but you feel he received his job without proper training. As a result, you have a tendency to be impatient with some of his decisions. For example, you supervise Joe's department much more closely than you do Mr. X's or Ms. Y's.

As Supervisor Joe you are the key personality in most Case Studies and Mini-Games. You consider yourself a hard-working, conscientious supervisor, but sometimes you feel insecure in your job. For about two years you were an employee in the department you now supervise. You know all the skills and techniques to teach others, but so far you have not been able to raise productivity as high as Mr. Big expects—and consequently you feel uneasy around Mr. Big. You are learning to delegate,

---

*Scramblers are highly motivated, unorthodox people who zigzag from one organization to another to get to the top; stabilizers are loyal, hard-working people who prefer to stay with a single organization and take a straight line to the top.

manage your time, and build good relationships with your people, but you realize you are still in a transition stage.

You are twenty-four years old and your wife works as a secretary. There are no children. You earned a degree from a two-year community college where you concentrated on business courses. You are a car buff who likes to restore antique automobiles.

People seem to react quickly and favorably to your warm personality and friendly attitude. As far as you can tell, all five of your employees like and respect you. You feel they come to you without fear to discuss problems of all kinds. You strive for a department that is happy and free of conflict. Mr. Big has recently told you to exercise stronger leadership and to distance yourself from your employees so they will learn to respect you more. Mr. X seems to resent your personal progress and frequently interferes in the operation of your department. Ms. Y also seems highly critical of you at times.

You look upon your job as a stepping-stone to middle management. In fact, you have already started to study Mr. Big and his job, because you feel his position is the next one up the ladder for which you must qualify. You recognize that you would be in a better position if you had graduated from a four-year college instead of a two-year institution, but you feel you can make up the difference with extra performance. You are thinking about taking some night courses that will lead to a four-year degree.

(NOTE: Ms. Y is a typical Theory Y supervisor—that is, one who operates on a low-key and somewhat permissive basis but nevertheless often achieves high productivity.)

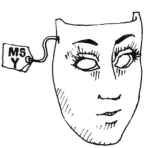

As Ms. Y you are a recent college graduate who believes in participative management. You involve your employees in departmental decisions when possible and pride yourself on your sensitivity to individual needs. You have developed your own informal communications system. You are assertive in your manner and consider yourself a scrambler rather than a stabilizer. Although you do not intend to stay with your present firm more than two years, you will not move until another employer offers you a substantial increase in your salary. You like the idea of becoming a top executive. So far your personnel turnover has been lower than in Mr. X's department, and your productivity is as high as his.

You are single, like to ski, and enjoy the challenges of work. You are self-motivated. You persistently study the leadership styles of others. You like Supervisor Joe but feel he is uninformed and clumsy. You feel Mr. X is much too demanding and a poor listener. You sense a deep conflict between your style and his. You intend to learn as much as possible from Mr. Big even though you have no intention of staying under his supervision long.

(NOTE: Mr. X represents the Theory X style of leadership. Mr. X is therefore painted as authoritarian and demanding, but fair. His controls are strict and definite.)

As Mr. X you have been with the organization longer than many others, including Mr. Big. It is your opinion that employees feel more secure and produce more under a firm and predictable discipline line.

Certainly you expect some conformity and high productivity from your employees, but they always know where they stand and they respect you for it. Although you believe in control more than participative management, you respect the people who work for you and treat them as individuals.

You supervise one of the departments located next to Supervisor Joe's. The two of you must work together closely to achieve the productivity goals set by management. You feel superior to Joe for three reasons: (1) you have twenty years more experience, (2) you helped the company through some tough times, thereby demonstrating your loyalty, (3) you have trained many people who are now in upper-management positions.

You feel that you are the supervisor best qualified to succeed Mr. Big, and you take advantage of every opportunity to demonstrate that you are ready for the job. You are rather proud that others feel you are a demanding supervisor. It works for you, and management knows it. All this attention to modern psychology in order to motivate people is not your style. You have let everybody know that you think Ms. Y and Joe are too people-oriented, too permissive, and too friendly with their employees. You didn't go to college—but who did in your day? Besides, in management, experience is the best teacher.

As Mr. K you have seniority over all the other employees in Joe's department. In fact, you have served under five different supervisors. You are married and have five children. Two are outstanding students in the local high school.

You feel you are a loyal, friendly, helpful employee, but you see no reason to extend yourself. You manage to keep your productivity at a safe average, and that is about as far as you intend to go. Joe is an O.K. supervisor (no better or worse than some of the other young ones you've adjusted to), but he probably won't last too long, so why worry. After all, you taught him most of what he knows about the job, and he still comes to you for advice.

You could have become department supervisor some years ago, but you turned it down because you didn't want the people problems involved. You feel the pay is fairly good and the benefits are great, so you coast along.

As Mrs. R you classify yourself as a re-entry "scrambler"—you will not be contented to mark time and wait for advancement. You are thirty-six years of age but entered the labor market only two years ago, after your marriage failed. You have a sizable mortgage and two children to raise. Everyone can see that you are active socially, but you never talk about your private life. You are well groomed and able to communicate in a persuasive manner. People in management respect you.

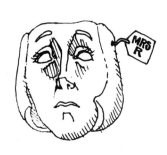

Although you had only two semesters of college, you know you are above average in intelligence. You learn quickly and are currently taking a course at the local community college in the elements of supervision. You become very impatient with Joe as a supervisor (as well as with other employees), but as yet you have said very little. You figure that if Joe stubs his toe or is moved up, you will be next in line. Meanwhile, if you sense a little hostility from your co-workers, you pass it off as unimportant. Your goal is to impress Supervisor Joe, Mr. Big, and their superiors.

Supervisor Joe and Mr. Big know that your personal productivity is substantially higher than that of others in the department, but you are not going to sit around and wait for further management recognition. You intend to promote yourself. Although you have been with the organization less than a full year, you hope to be the next supervisor, in either your own department or another one. If nothing happens soon, you will exercise your Plan B and move to a competitive organization at a higher salary.

As Mr. G you are black and twenty-eight years of age. You were raised in an inner-city neighborhood, but you seldom think about it anymore, because you have worked hard and now have a nice home and most things you need to lead the lifestyle you desire. Your wife works in a government job, and you have two children.

You were a high-school dropout some ten years ago, but you worked hard during your four-year hitch in the Marines and took an examination to receive your high school diploma. You are still weak in English and mathematics, but you have been going to adult evening classes to improve your proficiency in these two areas. Because of your advancement in the Marine Corps (you became a noncommissioned officer), you feel you have leadership ability.

You have earned the respect of Supervisor Joe, Mr. Big, and (you feel) all of your fellow employees except Mrs. R. You fully understand that you may have received a few breaks in the past, but you want to make it on your own from here on out. In fact, you hope to become a supervisor in a few months and perhaps qualify for Mr. Big's job a few years from now. You are next in line in terms of seniority after Mr. K, and you know he's not interested. You feel you are better qualified than Mrs. R for promotion because you are more sensitive to people and therefore have a stabilizing influence upon the department. Although you recognize that your personal productivity is not as high as Mrs. R's, you feel you contribute more than she does to the productivity of others.

As Mrs. Q you are twenty-three years old and have two years of college behind you. Everyone agrees you are good at your job. You like your job but it would not upset you should you be terminated tomorrow. You somehow feel you could get a better job if you really tried. You are seldom absent from work and never late. You know your productivity is above average but you also know it could be higher if you felt there was someplace to go in the organization. If a promotion came along now, either Mr. G or Mrs. R would get it, so why push? You recognize that you are not highly motivated and believe there is nothing management can do to change you.

Joe isn't the kind of guy you'd go all out for anyway. You think he is doing his best, but as far as you're concerned he doesn't understand people enough to get them really working together as a team. It's not the worst place in the world to work, though. The physical facilities are excellent, and the pay is O.K. At this point you are making slightly more money than your husband.

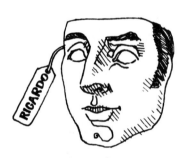

As Ricardo you are the only part-time employee in the department. You work twenty hours a week while taking a full program at a local college. You are nineteen and come from a large Mexican-American family. You are very handsome, a mod dresser, and are the first member of your family to go to college. You like the company and Supervisor Joe, but after you get your degree, you are going to look elsewhere.

You like your job because of the good pay, but it seems most of the dirty work is left for you to do. The company attitude appears to be that as long as you are a student, you don't really count and should be happy to do anything available. You resent this; so whenever you get a chance to speak up in a staff or group meeting, you do not hesitate to do so. After all, even though you are only part-time, you still have a right to be heard.

Supervisor Joe has been good about changing your work schedule so that you can attend classes. You feel, however, that the full-time employees take advantage of you, and you welcome any opportunity to voice your feelings.

Now that you are familiar with the nine roles, the Mini-Games and Case Problems should provide more intrigue, meaning, and value whether or not you receive the opportunity to discuss them in a classroom or seminar. If you are using this book for individualized study, treat the Mini-Games as cases and devise your own solutions. In a classroom or workshop the teacher or trainer will provide further instructions on how to play the Mini-Games.

# SRA Order Form

**Ship to:**

**Sold to:** (If different from shipping address)

_____
Date                          SRA Account Number

_____
SRA Account Number

_____
Purchase Order Number

_____
Account Name

_____
Ordered By

_____
Address

_____
Account Name

_____
City, State, Zip Code

_____
Address

_____
Attention

_____
City, State, Zip Code

_____
Telephone Number            Good time to reach

_____
Attention

_____
Tax Exemption Number

_____
Telephone Number            Good time to reach

_____
Preferred Delivery Method

☐ Charge to my: ☐ Visa ☐ MasterCard

[ ][ ][ ][ ][ ][ ][ ][ ][ ][ ][ ][ ][ ][ ]   [ ][ ][ ][ ]
Credit card account number              Expiration

_____
Cardholder's Signature

| Quantity* | SRA Product# | Product Name | Unit Price | Extension |
|-----------|--------------|--------------|------------|-----------|
|           |              |              |            |           |
|           |              |              |            |           |
|           |              |              |            |           |
|           |              |              |            |           |
|           |              |              |            |           |
|           |              |              |            |           |
|           |              |              |            |           |
|           |              |              |            |           |
|           |              |              |            |           |
|           |              |              |            |           |

*When product number refers to a set or package containing multiple copies, write the numbers of sets or packages you want us to send.

**The minimum order is $10.00, excluding shipping and taxes. Orders for less than $10.00 will be billed at the minimum order price.

**Individual Purchasers** Enclose full remittance with your order, including price of materials (calculated at list price), taxes, and shipping charges. (For shipping, add 5 percent of total price of materials or $1.00–whichever is greater.)

All orders are offers to purchase, subject to acceptance or rejection by SRA in Chicago, Illinois, in accordance with SRA's published terms and conditions of sale.

| | |
|---|---|
| Tax If Applicable | |
| | |
| Shipping Charges (Individuals) | |
| **Total | |

SRA
P.O. Box 5380
Chicago, IL 60680-5380